Mental Illness

OPPOSING VIEWPOINTS

I0967784

Other Books of Related Interest

Mental Illness

OPPOSING VIEWPOINTS

Tamara L. Roleff and Laura Egendorf, *Book Editors*

David L. Bender, *Publisher*
Bruno Leone, Executive *Editor*
Bonnie Szumski, *Editorial Director*
David M. Haugen, *Managing Editor*

OPPOSING
VIEWPOINTS®
SERIES

Greenhaven Press, Inc., San Diego, California

Cover photo: PhotoDisc, Inc.

Library of Congress Cataloging-in-Publication Data

Mental illness / Tamara L. Roleff, Laura K. Egendorf, book editors.
        p.   cm. — (Opposing viewpoints series)
    Includes bibliographical references and index.
    ISBN 0-7377-0348-2 (hc : alk. paper) —
ISBN 0-7377-0347-4 (pbk. : alk. paper)
    1. Mental illness—Public opinion. 2. Mental illness—Social
aspects. 3. Mental illness—Miscellanea. I. Roleff, Tamara L.,
1959–   . II. Egendorf, Laura K., 1973–   . III. Series.

RC454.4 .M463 2000
616.89—dc21   99-055632
                                                                    CIP

Greenhaven Press, Inc., P.O. Box 289009
San Diego, CA 92198-9009

"Congress shall make no law...abridging the freedom of speech, or of the press."

First Amendment to the U.S. Constitution

The basic foundation of our democracy is the First Amendment guarantee of freedom of expression. The Opposing Viewpoints Series is dedicated to the concept of this basic freedom and the idea that it is more important to practice it than to enshrine it.

Contents

Chapter 3: What Mental Health Issues Do Children Face?

Chapter 4: What Mental Health Treatments Are Beneficial?

Why Consider Opposing Viewpoints?

"The only way in which a human being can make some approach to knowing the whole of a subject is by hearing what can be said about it by persons of every variety of opinion and studying all modes in which it can be looked at by every character of mind. No wise man ever acquired his wisdom in any mode but this."

John Stuart Mill

In our media-intensive culture it is not difficult to find differing opinions. Thousands of newspapers and magazines and dozens of radio and television talk shows resound with differing points of view. The difficulty lies in deciding which opinion to agree with and which "experts" seem the most credible. The more inundated we become with differing opinions and claims, the more essential it is to hone critical reading and thinking skills to evaluate these ideas. Opposing Viewpoints books address this problem directly by presenting stimulating debates that can be used to enhance and teach these skills. The varied opinions contained in each book examine many different aspects of a single issue. While examining these conveniently edited opposing views, readers can develop critical thinking skills such as the ability to compare and contrast authors' credibility, facts, argumentation styles, use of persuasive techniques, and other stylistic tools. In short, the Opposing Viewpoints Series is an ideal way to attain the higher-level thinking and reading skills so essential in a culture of diverse and contradictory opinions.

In addition to providing a tool for critical thinking, Opposing Viewpoints books challenge readers to question their own strongly held opinions and assumptions. Most people form their opinions on the basis of upbringing, peer pressure, and personal, cultural, or professional bias. By reading carefully balanced opposing views, readers must directly confront new ideas as well as the opinions of those with whom they disagree. This is not to simplistically argue that everyone who reads opposing views will—or should—change his or her opinion. Instead, the series enhances readers' understanding of their own views by encouraging confrontation with opposing ideas. Careful examination of others' views can lead to the readers' understanding of the logical inconsistencies in their own opinions, perspective on why they hold an opinion, and the consideration of the possibility that their opinion requires further evaluation.

Evaluating Other Opinions

To ensure that this type of examination occurs, Opposing Viewpoints books present all types of opinions. Prominent spokespeople on different sides of each issue as well as well-known professionals from many disciplines challenge the reader. An additional goal of the series is to provide a forum for other, less known, or even unpopular viewpoints. The opinion of an ordinary person who has had to make the decision to cut off life support from a terminally ill relative, for example, may be just as valuable and provide just as much insight as a medical ethicist's professional opinion. The editors have two additional purposes in including these less known views. One, the editors encourage readers to respect others' opinions—even when not enhanced by professional credibility. It is only by reading or listening to and objectively evaluating others' ideas that one can determine whether they are worthy of consideration. Two, the inclusion of such viewpoints encourages the important critical thinking skill of objectively evaluating an author's credentials and bias. This evaluation will illuminate an author's reasons for taking a particular stance on an issue and will aid in readers' evaluation of the author's ideas.

As series editors of the Opposing Viewpoints Series, it is our hope that these books will give readers a deeper understanding of the issues debated and an appreciation of the complexity of even seemingly simple issues when good and honest people disagree. This awareness is particularly important in a democratic society such as ours in which people enter into public debate to determine the common good.

Those with whom one disagrees should not be regarded as enemies but rather as people whose views deserve careful examination and may shed light on one's own.

Thomas Jefferson once said that "difference of opinion leads to inquiry, and inquiry to truth." Jefferson, a broadly educated man, argued that "if a nation expects to be ignorant and free . . . it expects what never was and never will be." As individuals and as a nation, it is imperative that we consider the opinions of others and examine them with skill and discernment. The Opposing Viewpoints Series is intended to help readers achieve this goal.

David L. Bender & Bruno Leone,
Series Editors

Greenhaven Press anthologies primarily consist of previously published material taken from a variety of sources, including periodicals, books, scholarly journals, newspapers, government documents, and position papers from private and public organizations. These original sources are often edited for length and to ensure their accessibility for a young adult audience. The anthology editors also change the original titles of these works in order to clearly present the main thesis of each viewpoint and to explicitly indicate the opinion presented in the viewpoint. These alterations are made in consideration of both the reading and comprehension levels of a young adult audience. Every effort is made to ensure that Greenhaven Press accurately reflects the original intent of the authors included in this anthology.

Introduction

"The incredible pessimism associated with schizophrenia has frustrated psychiatrists for a long time."
—Patrick D. McGorry, psychiatry professor,
Wall Street Journal, *August 25, 1999*

Matthew was preparing to take the entrance exam to law school in 1995 when he started seeing double. Subsequent medical exams revealed that he had a lesion on his brain. During the next eighteen months, Matthew began to suffer from stress, rages, and sleeplessness. He also found it difficult to concentrate and became withdrawn from his family and friends. Matthew's symptoms and his age at their onset are characteristic of schizophrenia and he was diagnosed with the disease.

Contrary to popular belief, people with schizophrenia do not have multiple personalities. Instead, they experience a change in their perception of reality. Hallucinations (in which the person hears, sees, smells, or feels something that is not actually present) and delusions (in which a person's false beliefs cannot be shaken by the truth) are two of the most common symptoms of schizophrenia. The third "positive" sign of schizophrenia is thought disorder, in which the words spoken by a schizophrenic make absolutely no sense to listeners. Other signs of schizophrenia are called "negative" symptoms and include social isolation and withdrawal, mood swings, an inability to derive pleasure, a decreased ability or willingness to speak, and the loss of memory, reasoning, and the ability to solve problems.

Males with schizophrenia usually start to show signs of the brain disorder while in their late teens to early twenties; women generally do not experience symptoms until their twenties and occasionally as late as thirty. About one percent of the population develops schizophrenia, but for people who have close relatives with schizophrenia, the chances of developing the disease are about one in ten.

Psychiatrists who treat schizophrenia rely primarily upon antipsychotic drugs to keep the disease and its symptoms under control. These drugs are separated into two categories: typical and atypical, each with its own actions on the brain and side effects. Typical antipsychotic drugs have been used since the 1950s and their side effects include involuntary muscle spasms, muscle rigidity, and restlessness. Atypical drugs appeared in the early 1990s, and although they are costlier than typical antipsychotic drugs, they have been rapidly gaining in popularity. The atypical drugs are effective at treating the "negative" symptoms of schizophrenia—the social isolation and withdrawal, mood swings, and apathy. However, the atypical drugs have side effects of their own—lethargy, weight gain, constipation, and a dangerous blood condition that can result in infection and death.

In addition, psychotherapy can help the patient and the patient's family understand and cope with the disease. Because of the drugs' debilitating side effects, schizophrenia patients are sometimes reluctant to continue taking their medication when they feel healthy. Without the drugs, though, the patients will suffer a schizophrenic episode from which they will never fully recover. Psychotherapy helps schizophrenia patients stay on their drug regimen.

Scientists are now working on a new option for treating schizophrenia—prevention. Matthew's younger brother Josh is participating in a clinical drug trial at Yale University that is studying whether aggressively treating a patient for schizophrenia before it is diagnosed can prevent the onset of the disease. The nineteen people included in the study have a high risk of developing schizophrenia. Like Josh, they have a close relative who has been diagnosed with schizophrenia. They have also started exhibiting early symptoms of the disease, such as confusion, suspiciousness or paranoid thinking, poor rapport with others, passivity or disinterest in social activities, and "flat" emotions. The participants are treated for one year with either Zyprexa, a new atypical drug that researchers hope will prevent the onset of the disease, or a placebo. They also undergo therapy. During the second year, the patients are taken off the drug and monitored to see if they develop schizophrenia. If any of the study volunteers do develop schizophrenia, they are immediately placed in a standard treatment program; researchers will examine the severity of their disease to determine if the preventive treatment had any effect in lessening the disorder's symptoms.

The theory behind the drug trial is to prevent damage to the brain before it occurs. Scientists believe that the brain undergoes massive changes during late adolescence and young adulthood, when schizophrenia normally appears. While these changes are harmless to most people, they can irreversibly damage the brain of those who are at risk of schizophrenia and thus bring on the disease. Antipsychotic drugs have been found to be effective in repairing some of the damage in diagnosed schizophrenia patients. Thomas H. McGlashan, a Yale psychiatry professor who is in charge of the two-year clinical trial, hopes that administering these drugs before the changes occur will prevent or reduce the damage in the brain. He believes researchers have "a limited opportunity" in which they can try to prevent the onset of the disease. Preliminary results from a similar early-intervention study in Australia conducted by University of Melbourne psychiatry professor Patrick D. McGorry have found that none of the patients who took the antipsychotic drug Risperdal developed schizophrenic symptoms, while over one-third of those who were not given the drug developed symptoms.

There are several areas of concern about McGlashan's study, however. Many of the warning signs of schizophrenia are typical adolescent behaviors or may be indicators of other mental illnesses. For example, moodiness, withdrawal, apathy, and difficulty in concentrating may be normal teen behavior or symptoms of depression rather than signs of schizophrenia.

Some researchers also believe it is risky and dangerous to give powerful drugs to adolescents and young people whose brains are still developing. While David Lewis, a professor of psychiatry and neuroscience at the University of Pittsburgh Medical School, is excited about the prospect of preventing schizophrenia, he believes "the basic science that supports it is limited." He adds, "We need to be concerned about unintended adverse effects that may occur if interventions are made at a young age." Lewis points out that the effects of the drugs on developing healthy brains is unknown, as are any possible effects on the patients later in life.

New treatments for mental illness are constantly being proposed, administered, and studied. Psychiatrists, researchers, and scientists like McGlashan hope that perhaps one day mental illness can be prevented or even cured instead of just being treated for its symptoms as is done now. The viewpoints in the following chapters examine the effectiveness of methods used to treat mental disorders as well as the prevalence of mental illness in the following chapters: How Should Mental Illness Be Defined? How Should Society Deal with the Mentally Ill? What Mental Health Issues Do Children Face? and What Mental Health Treatments Are Beneficial? In these chapters, the authors give some perspective on the social, legal, and medical issues facing the mentally ill.

CHAPTER 1

How Should Mental Illnesses Be Defined?

Chapter Preface

The line separating mental health from mental illness is not always clear and distinct. Underlying the debate about what should be considered a mental illness is the question of whether mental illnesses are in fact medical diseases.

Several studies appear to support the argument that mental illnesses are medical diseases. For example, one study found definite differences between the brains of the mentally ill and the mentally healthy. According to psychiatrist Sheldon H. Preskorn, brain-imaging studies of mentally ill patients have demonstrated lesions and other disturbances in the brain structure and/or functions as well as biochemical changes that are not visible in the brains of individuals who do not show symptoms of mental illness. Further proof of the medical basis of mental illness, Preskorn contends, is the fact that treatment is effective for many mental illnesses.

However, critics of this theory claim that defining mental illness as a medical disease is merely an attempt by the psychiatric profession to justify its existence. Thomas Szasz, a longtime critic of psychiatry, refutes the theory that mental illness is the result of a genetic brain defect or lesion. According to Szasz, the mind is not an organ, and therefore it cannot be diseased:

> If mental illnesses are diseases of the central nervous system, then they are diseases of the brain, not the mind. And if mental illnesses are the names of (mis)behaviors, then they are behaviors, not diseases.

Therefore, Szasz continues, mental illness is a "myth" that enables people to evade responsibility for their problems and actions.

The concept of whether mental illness is a medical disease reflects the controversy over the prevalence of the disease. The authors in the following chapter debate whether mental illness is too broadly defined and whether certain behaviors should be considered mental illness.

"A mental illness would be anything the psychiatric profession chose to call a mental illness."

Mental Illness Is Too Broadly Defined

L.J. Davis

The *Diagnostic and Statistical Manual of Mental Disorders* (*DSM*), compiled and published by the American Psychiatric Association (APA), is a complete reference book of mental disorders and illnesses. L.J. Davis argues in the following viewpoint that according to the *DSM*, all types of perfectly normal behavior are classified as mental disorders. Many of these so-called psychiatric disorders are the result of physical diseases, he maintains, that should be treated by doctors who specialize in hard science. Furthermore, Davis contends that the APA's reason for identifying all these behaviors as mental disorders is to earn fees for its practitioners. Davis is a contributing editor to *Harper's Magazine*.

As you read, consider the following questions:
1. To what three things does Davis compare the *DSM*?
2. How many mental disorders were described in *DSM-I*, according to the author?
3. What belief does Davis claim is overlooked by the authors of the *DSM*?

Excerpted from "The Encyclopedia of Insanity," by L.J. Davis, *Harper's Magazine*, February 1997. Copyright ©1997 by Harper's Magazine. All rights reserved. Reprinted with the permission of *Harper's Magazine*.

Has there ever been a task more futile than the attempt to encompass, in the work of a single lifetime, let alone in a single work, the whole of human experience? For roughly five thousand years, poets, playwrights, philosophers, and cranks have incinerated untold quantities of olive oil, beeswax, and fossil fuel in pursuit of this maddeningly elusive goal; all have failed, sometimes heroically. Not even Shakespeare could manage it; closer to our own times, Dickens, a sentimental Englishman, the son of a clerk, perhaps came closest, though he believed in spontaneous human combustion and managed to miss the entirety of the twentieth century. Despite the best efforts of minds great, small, and sometimes insane, the riddle of the human condition has remained utterly impervious to solution. Until now. According to the *Diagnostic and Statistical Manual of Mental Disorders, Fourth Edition* (popularly known as the *DSM-IV*), human life is a form of mental illness.

Published by the American Psychiatric Association in 1994, the *DSM-IV* is some 886 pages long and weighs (in paperback) slightly less than three pounds; if worn over the heart in battle, it would probably stop a .50-caliber machine-gun bullet at 1,700 yards. Nearly a decade in the making, it is the product of work groups, task forces, advisers, and review committees (the acknowledgment of whom requires twenty-two pages) representing the flower of the profession and the distillation of its thought. The *DSM-IV* has no beginning, no middle, and no end; like a cookbook (which the preface is at pains to say it is not), the manual is organized by categories, not chapters. But it does have a plot (everyone is either nuts or going there), a central and unifying thesis (everyone is treatable), and it tells its stark tale with implacable simplicity. Here, on a staggering scale, are gathered together all the known mental disturbances of humankind, the illnesses of mind and spirit that cry out for the therapeutic touch of—are you ready for this?—the very people who wrote the book.

A Book of Dogma

First, and primarily, the *DSM-IV* is a book of dogma, though as theology it is pretty pedestrian stuff, rather along the lines of the owner's manual in an automobile glove compartment. Like all theories-of-everything, from the *Protocols of the Elders of Zion* to the collected lyrics of Mr. Snoop Doggy Dogg, the language is simultaneously precise and vague. The precision, which arrives in cool, clinical, and occasionally impenetrable language, provides the undertaking with an aura of scientific objectivity, and the vagueness is necessary because precision can be limiting in both a semantic and a financial sense. Secondly, the *DSM-IV* is a catalogue. The merchandise consists of the psychiatric disorders described therein, the customers are the therapists, and this may be the only catalogue in the world that actually makes its customers money: each disorder, no matter how trivial, is accompanied by a billing code, enabling the therapist to fill out the relevant insurance form and receive an agreed-upon reward. The billing code for Encopresis ("repeated passage of feces into inappropriate places"), for instance, is 307.7. Last, the manual bears an astounding resemblance to a militia's Web page, insofar as it constitutes an alternative reality under siege. The enemy, of course, is hard science and her white-coated thugs, who have long maintained that many psychiatric disorders do not exist and that others are physical diseases with mental consequences. Worse, things have been going hard science's way in recent years, which threatens no small number of soft-science incomes. The *DSM-IV*, then, may be read as a counterattack along the lines of a fertilizer bomb.

Perhaps some examples are in order. According to the *DSM-IV*, something called frotteurism (302.89) is the irresistible desire to sexually touch and rub against one's fellow passengers on mass transit. Something called fugue (300.13) consists of travel in foreign lands, often under an assumed identity. In reality, it may very well be that the frotteurist is a helpless victim in the clutches of his obsession, but it's equally possible that he's simply a bored creep looking for a cheap thrill. Perhaps the fuguist is in psychological flight from a memory that cannot be borne and will utterly fail to welcome the news that he is not the Regent of Pomerania traveling incognito in Provence, but maybe he's just having his spot of fun. The *DSM-IV* is a stranger to such ambiguities. The *DSM-IV* says that the frotteurist and the fuguist, despite all conceivable arguments to the contrary, have lost their marbles, period and end of discussion.

Every Action Is a Symptom

Not content with the merely weird, the *DSM-IV* also attempts to claim dominion over the mundane. Current among the many symptoms of the deranged mind are bad writing (315.2, and its associated symptom, poor handwriting); coffee drinking, including coffee nerves (305.90), bad coffee nerves (292.89), inability to sleep after drinking too much coffee (292.89), and something that probably has something to do with coffee, though the therapist can't put his finger on it (292.9); shyness (299.80, also known as Asperger's Disorder); sleepwalking (307.46); jet lag (307.45); snobbery (301.7, a subset of Antisocial Personality Disorder); and insomnia (307.42); to say nothing of tobacco smoking, which includes both getting hooked (305.10) and going cold turkey (292.0). You were out of your mind the last time you had a nightmare (307.47). Clumsiness is now a mental illness (315.4). So is playing video games (Malingering, V65.2). So is doing just about anything "vigorously." So, under certain circumstances, is falling asleep at night.

The foregoing list is neither random nor trivial, nor does it represent the sort of editorial oversight that occurs when, say, an otherwise reputable zoology text contains the claim that goats breathe through their ears. We are here confronted with a worldview where everything is a symptom and the predominant color is a shade of therapeutic gray. This has the advantage of making the therapist's job both remarkably simple and remarkably lucrative. Once the universe is populated with enough coffee-guzzling, cigarette-puffing, vigorous human beings who are crazy precisely because they smoke, drink coffee, and move about in an active and purposeful manner, the psychoanalyst is placed in the position of the lucky fellow taken to the mountaintop and shown powers and dominions. Here, hard science cannot attack with its niggling discoveries about bad brain chemicals and their effects on people who believe that gunplay is a perfectly reasonable response to disapproval, humor, or minor traffic accidents. Instead, the pages of the *DSM-IV* are replete with mental illnesses that have been hitherto regarded as perfectly normal behavior. The therapist is invited not merely to play God but to play lawyer—to some minds, a superior calling—and to indulge in a favorite diversion of the American legal profession known as "recruiting a fee.". . .

The History of the *DSM*

As recently as 1840, the U.S. census recognized precisely one form of madness, idiocy/insanity, omitting a definition because, presumably, everyone knew what it was. (In the 1840s, however, southern alienists anticipated the *DSM-IV* by discovering a malady called Drapetomania—the inexplicable, mad longing of a slave for freedom.) The 1880 census obligingly followed the march of science by listing no fewer than seven categories of dementia: mania, melancholia, monomania, paresis, dementia (again), dipsomania, and epilepsy. (This would not be the last time that a bald-facedly physical affliction crept into the psychological canon; among the maladies described in the *DSM-IV* is snoring, 780.59.) Even so, it cannot be said that the profession's urge to colonize the human mind proceeded at a blinding pace. The term "mental illness" did not enter the vocabulary for another forty years. Many decades would pass, and much caution would be thrown to the winds, before things began to get really out of hand.

Following World War II, the U.S. Army and the Veterans Administration revisited the timeless discovery that the experience of battle did unpleasant things to the minds of its luckless participants. As a result, the number of known mental disturbances grew to a still-reasonable twenty-six. The *DSM-I* appeared in 1952; it was the first professional manual that attempted to describe, in a single concise volume, the disorders a clinician might encounter in the course of daily practice. The *DSM-I* also described the disorders as actual, discernible reactions to something—an event, a situation, a biological condition. But when the *DSM-II* was published in 1968, the word "reaction" had vanished, never to reappear. Unobserved by the larger world, a revolution had taken place. By severing cause from effect, the psychiatric profession had privatized the entire field of mental illness, removed it from the marketplace of ideas, abandoned the rigorous proofs of the scientific method, and adopted circular thinking as its central discipline. Henceforward, in the absence of cause and effect, a mental illness would be anything the psychiatric profession chose to call a mental illness. Increasingly, and with gathering speed, American psychiatry came to resemble a man with a hammer.

A Disease Once, but Not Now

A defining moment, both for the profession and for the country, arrived with the publication in 1974 of the revised edition of the *DSM-II*, which abolished homosexuality as a mental illness. This was heartening news for a great many people, but they weren't quite off the hook. When the *DSM-III* was published in 1980, the world was informed that *believing* one's homosexuality to be a mental illness was now a mental illness (Ego-dystonic Homosexuality, 302), regardless, apparently, of where that belief might have originated.

Life Is a Mental Disorder

Brand new diseases, including a lot of implausible ones, are an old story for psychiatrists and their professional bible, the *Diagnostic and Statistical Manual of Mental Disorders*. The *DSM* has been revised many times, usually with a few old diseases thrown out and a large number of new ones tossed in. Among those added over the years have been caffeine-induced anxiety disorder, inhalant abuse, and telephone scatalogia (making heavy-breathing sexual phone calls). . . .

It's easy enough to make fun of all this, but there is a serious problem here. The *DSM* is converting nearly all life's stresses and bad habits into mental disorders. Almost everything we feel or do is listed somewhere in the *DSM* as an indicator of some dread disorder. This has the effect of creating and trying to enforce social values on the basis of scientific evidence that most people in the field admit is rather weak and unconvincing.

John Leo, *U.S. News & World Report*, October 27, 1997.

For years, countless numbers of other people continued to be told that they suffered from a crippling disorder called dementia praecox, that women experienced penis envy, and that schizophrenia was caused by bad parents. By the time the *DSM-IV* rolled around, all these former truths were inoperative, bad luck indeed to the thousands who had been convinced, in defiance of their senses, that they were either hopelessly off their chumps, rotten human beings, or both. The fact that so many people had been treated, punished, or stigmatized for conditions and circumstances that did not exist failed to suggest to the public at large that modern psychotherapy had no idea what mental illness was. Nor did the tumbrels roll when the psychiatric profession went on to discover (and make a bundle from) two entirely new nation-threatening epidemics for which no empirical proof exists: chronic depression (based on the readily observable fact that a whole lot of people, including people with serious or potentially fatal diseases, don't feel so hot about their lives) and suppressed memory. The profession had discovered a truth as old as the Republic: no one ever went broke by turning a mote into a beam.

Physical Problems as Mental Illnesses

It's one thing for the psychological profession to defend itself against the onslaught of physical medicine and quite another for it to go on the attack. In a widespread and disturbing tit for tat, the *DSM-IV* displays a tendency to claim dominion over afflictions that are clearly best handled by the harder scientists. Leaving aside such suspect entries as psychotic disorder caused by a physical illness (293.82) and Vaginismus (306.51), a look at the section entitled "Pain Disorder" is instructive. Pain Disorder comes in two billable forms: Pain Disorder Associated with Psychological Factors (307.80) and Pain Disorder with Both Psychological Factors and a General Medical Condition (307.89). Its variant form—Pain Disorder Associated with a General Medical Condition—seems to cede ground to the physicians, but subsequent text plainly reveals this to be a snare and an illusion:

> Pain may lead to inactivity and social isolation, which in turn can lead to additional psychological problems (e.g., depression) and a reduction in physical endurance that results in fatigue and additional pain.

On the small chance that this bit of legerdemain does not suffice, the text goes on to hint less subtly:

The associated mental disorders may precede the Pain Disorder (and possibly predispose the individual to it), co-occur with it, or result from it.

If your knee hurts, in other words, you have bats in your belfry.

Even when a problem has admittedly physical origins, the *DSM-IV* manages to argue that it, too, is treatable by the adepts of the psychological craft. With an audacity that would be shameless in another context, the book devotes an entire section to the psychological maladies caused by drugs prescribed to alleviate other, perhaps imaginary, psychological maladies. This is a little bit like receiving a bill from a virus. Elsewhere, the manual's logic shows a similar taste for the absurd, devoting almost a hundred pages to the discovery that chronic intoxication (a matter of keen interest to the *DSM-IV*) results from the ingestion of intoxicating substances (a matter of no visible interest to the *DSM-IV*) and often results in (but is not caused by) both crime and poverty. The poor, by the way, frequently suffer from impoverished vocabularies (Expressive Language Disorder, 315.31).

Childhood Mental Illnesses

Nowhere is this strange conflation of cause and effect on more prominent display than in the passage entitled Reactive Attachment Disorder in Infancy or Early Childhood (313.89). "The child," we are informed,

> shows a pattern of excessively inhibited, hypervigilant, or highly ambivalent responses (e.g., frozen watchfulness, resistance to comfort, or a mixture of approach and avoidance). . . . By definition, the condition is associated with grossly pathological care that may take the form of persistent disregard of the child's basic emotional needs for comfort, stimulation, and affection. . . .

Thirty-five thousand years of human history says that the kid is reacting logically to an intolerable situation. The *DSM-IV* says that the kid, like the drunk and the poor person, is not playing with a full deck. Neither is any other kid who hits the hormonal wall in the mid-teens, a condition well known to generations of parents whose darkest suspicions are confirmed by the *DSM-IV*'s version of the scientific method. Under the heading of "Disorders Usually First Diagnosed in Infancy, Childhood, or Adolescence," the *DSM-IV* lists Attention-Deficit/Hyperactivity Disorder (314.00, 314.01, and 314.9), Conduct Disorder (312.8), Oppositional Defiant Disorder (313.81), and Disruptive Behavior Disorder Not Otherwise Specified (312.9). A close reading of the text reveals that the illnesses in question consist of failure to listen when spoken to, talking back, annoying other people, claiming that somebody else did it, and (among a lot of other stuff familiar to parents) failure to clean up one's room. According to the *DSM-IV*, adolescence is a mental disorder.

A Disclaimer

At this point in the proceedings it is time for the standard author's disclaimer. First, a number, perhaps even a large number, of practicing therapists are sensible, upstanding citizens who never cheat on their expense accounts and who know perfectly well that poor people aren't crazy. The problem is finding out who these therapists are. The *DSM-IV* lists as contributors many of the most stellar names in the profession, and the daunting task of weeding out misguided, deluded, corrupt, or stupid therapists doesn't even begin to address the legions of social workers, lawyers, nurses, administrators, and jumped-up file clerks who use the *DSM-IV* as a kind of Cliffs Notes while filling out paperwork and blackening countless reputations with descriptions of illnesses that do not exist.

Next, and obviously, there actually is such a thing as mental illness. Any form of normal human thought or behavior carried to a grotesque extreme and persisting despite all appeals to reason is, by definition, a mental illness. The *DSM-IV*, however, appears to be unaware of this. The manual's lengthy discussion of schizophrenia (295.30, 295.10, 295.20, 295.90, and 295.60), surely one of the most studied pathologies ever to afflict the mind of man, boils down to this: a schizophrenic is a person who thinks very odd thoughts, behaves weirdly, and suffers from bizarre delusions, which suggests that the authors of the *DSM-IV* either don't know what schizophrenia is or suffer from poor writing skills (315.2). Hard science has developed compelling evidence that schizophrenia, like appendicitis, is not something that its victims can be talked out of, but one begins to suspect that the entire strangely imprecise section has been composed with the wisdom of the serpent: if the *DSM-IV* were to admit that schizophrenia is in all probability a physical illness with profound mental consequences, then the game would no longer be worth the candle.

Overlooked Mental Illnesses

Nowhere in the *DSM-IV* is a state of sanity defined or described, and a therapist is therefore given no guidance concerning therapy's goal. In the *DSM-IV*'s own terms, sanity appears to be the absence of everything in its pages. And for all their effort to sweep every known disturbance of mankind under psychology's jurisdictional rug, the book's authors seem to have overlooked a few real moneymakers. A number of people believe, for example, that they have been abducted by intergalactic superbeings and subjected to fiendish experiments, but because the *DSM-IV* never describes this condition, there is nothing at all wrong with such people. A person who snores or travels incognito is ready for the booby hatch, but a person who claims to have been kidnapped by a flying saucer is perfectly sane.

Well, almost. Perhaps he is "agitated," in which case it would be reasonable to treat him for "agitation" (and bill his insurance company accordingly). Is he depressed about the incident? If so, perhaps he has gone Bipolar. And the saucer story could, of course, be read as a schizophrenic delusion. The possibilities are various.

This, in the end, is the beauty of the *DSM-IV*. Hangnails seem to have avoided the amoeba's kiss, and the common cold is momentarily safe (unless it is accompanied by pain), but precious little else is. As psychiatry refines its definitions with an eye toward profit, piling Pelion on Ossa like a playwright dressing a set, the human mind becomes increasingly less comprehensible, not more. If every aspect of human life (excepting, of course, the practice of psychiatry) can be read as pathology, then everything human beings thought they knew, believed, or had deduced about their world is consigned to the dustbin of history or a line on an insurance form.

> *"An increased number of diagnoses does not mean . . . that more individuals are being diagnosed with mental illnesses. . . . More precise diagnoses significantly aid the advance of research and treatment."*

Mental Illness Is Not Too Broadly Defined

American Psychiatric Association

The Diagnostic and Statistical Manual of Mental Disorders (known as DSM or DSM-IV), is known as the "bible" of the psychiatric profession due to its complete listing of mental disorders recognized by doctors, therapists, and health insurers. In the following viewpoint, the American Psychiatric Association (APA), which compiles the DSM, defends the process in which mental diseases are added to the manual. A diagnosis cannot be based on the DSM alone, the APA argues; psychiatric training in the recognition and treatment of mental diseases is also essential to making an accurate diagnosis. The APA is an organization of psychiatrists dedicated to studying the nature, treatment, and prevention of mental disorders.

As you read, consider the following questions:
1. According to the APA, what steps do psychiatrists take to diagnose a mental disorder before consulting the DSM?
2. In the APA's view, how does increasing the number of mental disorders affect the diagnostic "pie" of individuals with mental illnesses?

Excerpted with permission from the *Diagnostic and Statistical Manual of Mental Disorders, Fourth Edition.* Copyright ©1994 by the American Psychiatric Association.

The American Psychiatric Association published a Fourth Edition of its *Diagnostic and Statistical Manual of Mental Disorders* in 1994. It replaced *DSM-III (Revised)*, which was published in 1987.

DSM-IV's Importance to Psychiatric Diagnosis

Diagnosis is the foundation of any medical practice, and the twentieth century has seen a revolution in medicine's ability to identify—and treat—the illnesses that plague humanity.

The practice of psychiatry—the medical specialty that treats mental illnesses—has been a major participant in this revolution, and indeed in the last four decades has seen it accelerate. Psychiatrists depend on accurate diagnostic tools to help them identify precisely the mental illnesses their patients suffer, an essential step in deciding what treatment or combination of treatments the patient needs. The American Psychiatric Association's *Diagnostic and Statistical Manual (DSM)*, in its four editions, has become a central part of this process. *DSM-IV* is based on decades of research and the input of thousands of psychiatric experts from across the country and in every sub-specialty. It has evolved into a carefully constructed, numerical index of mental illnesses grouped by categories and sub-categories. Each entry contains a general description of the disorder followed by a listing of possible symptoms, which enables clinicians to identify their patients' illnesses with a high degree of accuracy and confidence.

In addition to its utility as a diagnostic tool, the *DSM-IV*'s mental disorders coding helps in the process of research data collection and retrieval, and also helps as researchers compile information for statistical studies. The *DSM-IV*'s codes are in agreement with the *International Classification of Diseases, Ninth Edition, Clinical Modification (ICD-9-CM)*. *ICD-9-CM* is based on the *ICD-9*, a publication of the World Health Organization used worldwide to aid in consistent medical diagnoses. The *DSM-IV*'s codes often are required by insurance companies when psychiatrists, other physicians, and other mental health professionals file claims. The U.S. government's Health Care Financing Administration also requires mental health care professionals to use the codes for the purposes of Medicare reimbursement.

- *DSM-IV* was developed through an open process involving more than 1,000 national and international researchers and clinicians drawn from a wide range of mental and general health fields.

- *DSM-IV* is based on a systematic, empirical study of the evidence (consisting of literature reviews, data reanalyses, and field trials).

- *DSM-IV* is accompanied for the first time by a separate *Sourcebook* which carefully documents the rationale and empirical support for the text and criteria sets presented in *DSM-IV*.

- *DSM-IV* is clearly more specific and easier to use than previous versions. *DSM-IV* reflects an increased emphasis on the influence of culture, ethnicity, age, and gender on psychiatric assessment and diagnosis.

- *DSM-IV* reflects an increased emphasis on differential diagnosis and the role of substance use and general medical conditions in the development of psychiatric disorders.

How Psychiatrists and Other Mental Health Professionals Use *DSM-IV*

It is important to understand that psychiatrists and other mental health professionals do not use *DSM-IV* as a "cookbook" for psychiatric diagnosis. *DSM-IV* has been carefully written and exhaustively researched, but it cannot take the place of psychiatric training in the recognition and treatment of mental disorders and the clinician's informed judgment.

The process of diagnosis begins with the patient interview. Psychiatrists will order or conduct a careful general medical examination of each patient to assess his or her general health. They will request their patients' medical records from other physicians who've treated their patients. They will carefully question their patients about their past history and the symptoms of their disorder, the length of time they've had the symptoms, and their severity. If it seems warranted, the psychiatrist will also specify a period of observation. It is only after this careful assessment process that a psychiatrist will turn to the *DSM-IV*.

DSM-IV is organized according to phenomenology, that is, by groups of like symptoms which are commonly associated with a specific illness. Its descriptions of illnesses and lists of symptoms are meant to support the diagnostic process, providing clinicians with diagnostic guidelines, *not* a set of disorder "check lists."

As the number of psychiatric diagnoses has grown over time, researchers and clinicians have been able to share their knowledge of mental disorders with greater precision. An increased number of diagnoses does not mean, however, that more individuals are being diagnosed with mental illnesses. The diagnostic "pie" has not gotten larger; rather, the pieces of that pie have gotten smaller and more precise. More precise diagnoses significantly aid the advance of research and treatment.

The Importance of the Psychiatric Bible

On the shelf of every mental health professional is a copy of the *Diagnostics and Statistical Manual of Mental Disorders*. The American Psychiatric Association's 900-page reference book attempts to describe and classify each one of over 300 mental disorders. . . .

Part of the power of DSM derives from its attempt to distinguish mental disorder from other human troubles. Although to some laypeople the importance of the distinction may not be immediately clear, it is an enormously consequential one. DSM is a claim for professional jurisdiction by the American Psychiatric Association. The broadness of this claim provides justification for the scope of psychiatric expertise and a basis for requests for governmental and private support. But it does more: it proposes how we as a society should think about our troubles. By creating categories for certain behaviors, DSM determines which behaviors should be considered a result of illness or disorder and should therefore fall under the purview of psychiatrists and other mental health professionals. Mental disorder is, by definition, a matter of internal dysfunction, an indication that something harmful has gone wrong with a person's mental apparatus. Thus, to label specific behaviors as mental disorders, . . . is to instruct us to see the behavior as a direct result of a malfunction of the individual.

Herb Kutchins and Stuart A. Kirk, *Making Us Crazy*, 1997.

After analyzing the information gathered in the patient interview and from other sources in the context of the *DSM*, a psychiatrist makes a *preliminary* diagnosis. Even with an increased number of diagnoses available, there are few perfect fits in the diagnosis of any medical condition, because symptoms may vary from person to person, both in their type and severity. For this reason, experienced clinicians know that it is important to observe a patient and the patient's symptoms over time, and to sharpen the diagnosis using the information this observation provides.

Use of *DSM-IV* in Forensic Settings

When the *DSM-IV* categories, criteria, and textual descriptions are employed in making legal judgments, there are significant risks that diagnostic information will be misused or misunderstood. These dangers arise because of an imperfect fit between the questions of ultimate concern to the law and the information contained in a clinical diagnosis. For example, the inclusion in *DSM-IV* of diagnostic categories such as pedophilia or pathological gambling does not imply that these conditions meet legal or other non-medical criteria for what constitutes "mental disease," "mental disorder," or "mental disability." Many such terms, including "insanity" and "mental abnormality," are legal concepts, not medical ones. The clinical and scientific considerations involved in *DSM-IV*'s categorization of conditions as mental disorders may not be wholly relevant to legal judgments that take into account such issues as individual responsibility, disability determination, and competency.

When used appropriately, however, diagnoses and diagnostic information can assist legal decision makers in their determinations. *DSM-IV* can facilitate legal decision makers' understanding of the relevant characteristics of mental disorders. The literature related to diagnoses also serves as a check on ungrounded speculation about mental disorders and about the functioning of a particular individual.

Some History

The *DSM* had its origin in the Association's 1917 collaboration with the U.S. Bureau of the Census on a classification of mental illnesses that would enable the collection of uniform statistics on mental disorders seen in hospitals. The American Medical Association later expanded this classification system with its *Standard Classified Nomenclature of Disease*. During World War II, the U.S. armed forces medical services found these diagnostic criteria too restrictive, and developed a more expanded set, which was later revised for use by the Veterans Administration. In 1948, the World Health Organization (WHO) published its own diagnostic directory of mental illnesses as part of the sixth edition of its *International Classification of Diseases (ICD-6)*.

Users of these classification criteria found their differences confusing. Some used one system for clinical work, another to gauge levels of disability, and a third for statistical reporting. To rectify this situation, the APA began work on the document that would become *DSM*.

APA began with the military's diagnostic criteria, expanded them to create one system that could be used for diagnostic and statistical purposes, and included a glossary of definitions for the different illnesses the guide encompassed. APA brought the results of this work out as the first *DSM* in 1952.

As research has increased psychiatry's understanding of mental illnesses and sharpened its ability to diagnose and treat them, the *DSM* has changed to reflect this greater level of sophistication. APA published its second edition of the manual, *DSM-II*, in 1968. *DSM-III* came twelve years later, in 1980. APA published a major revision of this edition—*DSM-III* (Revised)—in 1987. *DSM-IV* was the next step in this continuing evolution.

The *DSM*'s Importance

The value of the *DSM* series to those researching and treating mental illnesses has grown through the years. It is now widely accepted in the United States as the common language of mental health clinicians and researchers for communicating about mental illnesses. Major textbooks of psychiatry and other textbooks that discuss psychopathology have made extensive reference to *DSM* and have largely adopted its terminology and concepts. It has been translated into Chinese, Danish, Dutch, Finnish, French, German, Greek, Hungarian, Italian, Japanese, Norwegian, Portuguese, Russian, Spanish, Swedish, Turkish and Ukrainian. In light of this widening currency, it is vital that the *DSM* undergo periodic updates so that it reflects the latest research findings and clinical practices.

How the *DSM-IV* Was Created

In managing the process that yielded *DSM-IV*, the APA tried to continue the pattern laid down by the preceding volumes, providing clear descriptions of diagnostic categories in order to enable clinicians and investigators to diagnose, communicate about, study and treat the various mental disorders.

According to Dr. Allen Frances, Chair of the *DSM-IV* Task Force, "The major innovation of *DSM-IV* lies not in any of its specific content changes, but rather in the systematic and explicit process by which it was constructed and documented. More than any other nomenclature of mental disorders, *DSM-IV* is grounded in empirical evidence."

The special 27-member *DSM-IV* Task Force worked for five years to develop the manual in a process that involved more than 1,000 psychiatrists and other mental health professionals. Under Dr. Frances's leadership, the task force developed thirteen work groups, each of which focused on a section of the manual. The work groups and each of their advisory groups of 50 to 100 individuals developed the manual in a three-step process.

The first step in the three-stage empirical review was the development of 150 reviews of the scientific literature which provided the empirical data base upon which *DSM-IV* decisions could be made. In the second step, task force work groups reanalyzed 50 separate sets of data which provided additional scientific information to that available in the published literature. These reanalysis projects were funded by the John D. and Catherine T. MacArthur Foundation.

Finally, the task force conducted twelve field trials with funding from the National Institute of Mental Health, National Institute on Drug Abuse, and the National Institution of Alcoholism and Alcohol Abuse, involving more than 88 sites in the United States and internationally, and evaluations of more than 7,000 patients. These field trials enabled one task force to evaluate the utility of alternate possible diagnostic criteria sets.

APA members and the mental health scientific community worldwide were kept informed of the manual's development from its inception through presentations at professional meetings; articles in the scientific literature; a special newsletter, *DSM-IV Update*; *APA's Psychiatric News*; and through publication in July 1991 of an "options book" which highlighted disorders or particular criteria being considered for revision.

The task force set high standards for evaluating proposals for changes in the new manual. Recommended changes had to be substantiated by explicit statements of rationale, supported by the systematic review of relevant empirical data.

The task force also published a multi-volume *DSM-IV Sourcebook*, which provides a comprehensive reference of the clinical and research data supporting the various decisions reached by the work groups and task force.

The manual defines a mental disorder as "a clinically significant behavioral or psychological syndrome or pattern that occurs in an individual and that is associated with present distress (a painful symptom) or disability (impairment in one or more important areas of functioning) or with a significantly increased risk of suffering death, pain or disability. In addition, this syndrome or pattern must not be merely an expectable and culturally sanctioned response to a particular event, e.g., the death of a loved one. Whatever its original cause, it must currently be considered a manifestation of a behavioral, psychological or biological dysfunction in the individual. Neither deviant behavior, e.g., political, religious, or sexual, nor conflicts that are primarily between the individual and society are mental disorders unless the deviance or conflict is a symptom of a dysfunction in the individual, as described above." The *DSM-IV* Task Force stresses that "a diagnosis does not carry any necessary implications regarding the causes of the individual's mental disorder or its associated impairments."

It is also important to note that in preparing *DSM-IV* APA also established a working relationship with the World Health Organization to clear up the differences between the new *DSM* and future versions of WHO's *International Classification of Diseases (ICD)*.

To make it easier for mental health professionals to use

DSM-IV in diagnosing people from diverse cultural and ethnic settings, *DSM-IV* includes a section in the text that covers culturally-related features. The section describes culturally-specific symptom patterns, the ways people from different cultural backgrounds will describe their psychiatric symptoms, and prevalence data when available. It provides the clinician with guidance on how a patient's cultural and ethnic background will influence the way he or she appears during a consultation. For example, in some cultures, depressive disorders are characterized more by physical symptoms than by feelings of sadness.

"[Mental illnesses] are real illnesses of a real organ—the brain."

Mental Illness Is a Disease

Hillary Rodham Clinton and Steven Hyman

In the following viewpoint, excerpted from their remarks at the White House Conference on Mental Health, First Lady Hillary Rodham Clinton and Steven Hyman, director of the National Institute of Mental Health, assert that mental illnesses are real and treatable diseases. According to the authors, scientists have proven that illnesses such as schizophrenia are illnesses of the brain. Consequently, they argue, mental illnesses should be treated similarly to general medical disorders, with medication and behavioral treatment.

As you read, consider the following questions:
1. What does Clinton believe is America's obligation regarding mental illness?
2. Which illnesses has science discovered to be genetic disorders, according to Hyman?
3. In addition to medication, what does Hyman also say works on the brain?

Excerpted from testimony given by Hillary Rodham Clinton and Steven Hyman to the White House Conference on Mental Health, June 7, 1999, Washington, D.C.

Hillary Clinton: This is an historic conference, but it is more than that; it's a real signal to our nation that we must do whatever it takes not only to remove the stigma from mental illness, but to begin treating mental illness as the illness it is on a parity with other illnesses. And we have to understand more about the progress that has been made scientifically that has really led us to this point.

A New Responsibility

I don't believe that we could have had such a conference even 10 years ago, and I know we couldn't have had such a conference 25 or 30 years ago, when I was a young law student working at the Child Study Center at the Yale University and taking classes at the Med School and working at the Yale New Haven Hospital, and very interested in the intersection of mental illness and the law and in the development of children and other issues that we were only then just beginning to address. And we didn't have a lot of evidence to back up what we needed to know or how we should proceed with the treatment of a lot of the problems that we saw.

Well, today we know a lot more. And it is really our obligation and responsibility, therefore, to begin to act on that scientific knowledge. And I'm very pleased to be talking with a distinguished group of panelists about the science of mental health and mental illness.

We're happy to have with us Dr. Steven Hyman. He is a distinguished scientist who directs the National Institute of Mental Health, one of the institutes of the National Institutes of Health. And I want to start with Doctor Hyman.

Dr. Hyman, you have been dealing with some very difficult diseases that affect millions of people. We've already heard several mentioned—clinical depression, bipolar disorder, schizophrenia. What progress have we made in learning about these diseases in the last few years so that we understand them more scientifically, and, therefore, have a better idea of what to do about them?

Real Illnesses

Steven Hyman: Well, Mrs. Clinton, the first thing that we've recognized is that the numbers are indeed enormous. More than 19 million Americans suffer from depression. More than 2 million children. More than 2 million Americans have schizophrenia. And the World Bank and the World Health Organization have recognized that depression is the leading cause of disability worldwide, including the United States.

We have also learned some very important facts about these illnesses, and if I can just encapsulate them briefly, it's that these are real illnesses of a real organ—the brain. Just like coronary artery disease is a disease of a real organ—the heart. We can make diagnoses, and these diseases are treatable.

In addition, we've learned that these diseases should be treated just like general medical disorders. If you have heart disease you would get not only medication, but also rehabilitation, dietary counseling, stress reduction. So it is with a mental illness. We've heard a lot already today about medication, but people need to get their medication in the context of appropriate psychotherapies and other psycho-social treatments.

Scientific Discoveries

Clinton: So how then have these scientific discoveries changed the way that we as a society deal with mental illness? And following up on what you said, if we now know—if you as experts and practitioners know that we should treat mental illness as real and as treatable, as a disease of a bodily part, namely the brain, what does that mean for the kind of response that we should be looking to in society?

Hyman: You know, sometimes people think of science as something cold, but actually it has been an enormously liberating force for families and for people with mental illness. Not two decades ago, people were taught that dread diseases like autism or schizophrenia were due to some subtle character flaw in mothers. This idea, unfortunately, has been perpetuated by ignorance far too often. And, indeed, these ideas didn't help with treatments. And what they did do is they demoralized families who ultimately had to take care of these poor sick children.

So science has shown us some alternative ideas. For example, it's turned out that autism, schizophrenia, manic-depressive illness are incredibly genetic disorders. What this means is that genes have an awful lot to say about whether somebody has one of these illnesses. And I have to tell you that as the human genome project approaches completion, in the next few years, we're going to be discovering the genes that create vulnerability to these disorders.

Depression Is a Disease

Many people—including many physicians—still mistake chemical imbalances for weakness of character and don't take the disease seriously. Even though depression takes a greater cumulative toll on society than, say, heart disease, it receives less than one tenth the federal funding. The very name depression, some contend, is responsible for much of the problem, because the word is misleading. "People confuse it with the everyday sensation of feeling despondent and dismiss it," says National Institute of Mental Health (NIMH) neuroscientist Philip Gold. "In fact, it takes an incredibly strong person to bear the burden of the disease, which ought to be given a more appropriate name." He suggests "hypothalamo-pituitary-adrenal axis dysfunction"—an appropriately jargony medical description that is accurate but would never make it into the headlines. At least 12 million people are now suffering from the disease without any treatment at all, some with the mistaken belief that one can will oneself to be well. For those who do seek help, it's not unusual to consult with as many as three doctors over 10 years just to get the right diagnosis—let alone an effective remedy.

Joannie M. Schrof and Stacey Schultz, *U.S. News & World Report*, March 8, 1999.

Now, that's important because genes are the blueprints of cells and by understanding those blueprints, I think we're going to come up with treatments that we could not possibly have dreamt of.

The other thing, as you mentioned, is we're learning an enormous amount about how the brain is built and how the brain operates. I brought a few pictures—I don't know if we can project them, but I think pictures are worth an awful lot. You can see on the left the brain of a healthy person, and on the right the brain of someone with schizophrenia, given a cognitive task that requires planning and holding something in mind. The kind of task that a person with schizophrenia has difficulty with. And what you can see just looking at the red spots, that people with schizophrenia don't activate their brain in the same way as a person without this illness.

Treating the Brain

We also know—and I think this is really interesting—if we could have the next slide—that our treatments work because they work on the brain. No one is surprised that medication works on the brain, but what we're learning is that psychotherapy also works on the brain. So what you can see in the lower two brain diagrams is that this is someone with an animal phobia—something that we can study relatively easily—before treatment. Now, after a cognitive behavioral treatment that exposes and desensitizes the person, you can see new spots of activity—they're shown in green—and they represent activation of our prefrontal cortex, a modern part of the brain—which is actually able to suppress some of the fear circuitry.

Now, I don't want to over-sell this, but ultimately we're going to understand how these treatments work in the brain.

And then, finally, I just want to show you a picture that is somewhat alarming, but what we see here on the left, someone with—a healthy person with a normal brain, and then on the right someone who has had severe depression for a long time. What you see outlined in red at the bottom is that a key structure acquired from memory—actually gets smaller, it deteriorates if depression is not treated.

Now, this is not so hopeless as it seems because we believe that with treatment these changes can be reversed. But I'm showing you these pictures again to remind us that these are real diseases of a real organ—the brain—that we can make diagnoses and that these should be treated just like general medical illnesses.

"Since the mind is not a physical organ, it cannot have a disease. While one can have a diseased brain, one cannot have a diseased mind."

Mental Illness Is Not a Disease

Martin Bobgan and Deidre Bobgan

Martin Bobgan and Deidre Bobgan argue in the following viewpoint that mental illness is not a disease. Although a brain can be diseased, the mind cannot, they contend, because the mind is not a physical organ. Bobgan and Bobgan assert that blaming mental, emotional, and behavioral problems on mental illness allows people to reject free will and personal responsibility for their actions. Behaviors typically described as mental illness are more accurately characterized as "problems of living," the authors maintain. Bobgan and Bobgan are the authors of *PsychoHeresy: The Psychological Seduction of Christianity* and codirectors of PsychoHeresy Awareness Ministries, an organization which believes that many concepts of psychological counseling are contrary to biblical beliefs.

As you read, consider the following questions:
1. What happens when a person's behavior is labeled as "illness," in the authors' opinion?
2. According to Bobgan and Bobgan, what is the purpose of the human mind?
3. Why is it erroneous to suggest that mental illnesses are actually brain diseases, according to E. Fuller Torrey as cited by the authors?

Reprinted from "Psychology: Science or Religion?" Special Report, *Media Spotlight*, 1999, condensed from *PsychoHeresy: The Psychological Seduction of Christianity*, by Martin Bobgan and Deidre Bobgan (Santa Barbara, CA: Eastgate Publishers, 1987). Reprinted with permission of the authors.

The terms *mental disease, mental illness,* and *mental disorder* are popular catch-alls for all kinds of problems of living, most of which have little or nothing to do with disease. As soon as a person's behavior is labeled "illness," treatment and therapy become the solutions. If, on the other hand, we consider a person to be responsible for his behavior, we should deal with him in the areas of education, faith, and choice. If we label him "mentally ill," we rob him of the human dignity of personal responsibility and the divine relationship by which problems may be met.

Examining the Accuracy of "Mental Illness"

Because the term *mental illness* throws attitudes and behavior into the medical realm, it is important to examine its accuracy. In discussing the concept of mental illness or mental disease, research psychiatrist E. Fuller Torrey says:

> The term itself is nonsensical, a semantic mistake. The two words cannot go together . . . you can no more have a mental "disease" than you can have a purple idea or a wise space.

The word mental means "mind" and the mind is not the same as the brain. Also, the mind is really more than just a function or activity of the brain. Brain researcher and author Barbara Brown insists that the mind goes beyond the brain. She says:

> The scientific consensus that mind is only mechanical brain is dead wrong . . . the research data of the sciences themselves point much more strongly toward the existence of a mind-more-than-brain than they do toward the mere mechanical brain action.

God created the human mind to know Him and to choose to love, trust, and obey Him. In the very creative act, God planned for mankind to rule His earthly creation and to serve as his representatives on earth. Because the mind goes beyond the physical realm, it goes beyond the reaches of science and cannot be medically sick.

Since the mind is not a physical organ, it cannot have a disease. While one can have a diseased brain, one cannot have a diseased mind, although he may have a sinful or unredeemed mind. Torrey aptly says:

> The mind cannot *really* become diseased any more than the

intellect can become abscessed. Furthermore, the idea that mental "diseases" are actually brain diseases creates a strange category of "diseases" which are, by definition, without known cause. Body and behavior become intertwined in this confusion until they are no longer distinguishable. It is necessary to return to first principles: a disease is something you *have*, behavior is something you do.

One can understand what a diseased body is, but what is a diseased mind? It is obvious that one cannot have a diseased emotion or a diseased behavior. Then why a diseased mind? Nevertheless, therapists continually refer to mental-emotional-behavioral problems as diseases.

The "Psychiatric Imposter"

Thomas Szasz criticizes what he calls the "psychiatric impostor" who "supports a common, culturally shared desire to equate and confuse brain and mind, nerves and nervousness." Not only are brain and mind not synonymous, neither are nerves and nervousness. One might nervously await the arrival of a friend who is late for an appointment, but the nerves are busy performing other tasks. Szasz further says:

> It is customary to define psychiatry as a medical specialty concerned with the study, diagnosis, and treatment of mental illness. This is a worthless and misleading definition. Mental illness is a myth . . . the notion of a person "having a mental illness" is scientifically crippling. It provides professional assent to the popular rationalization—namely, that problems in living experienced and expressed in terms of so-called psychiatric symptoms are basically similar to bodily diseases.

Although a medical problem or brain disease may bring on mental-emotional-behavioral symptoms, the person does not and cannot rationally be classified as "mentally ill." He is medically ill, not mentally ill. The words *psychological* and *biological* are not synonymous. In the same way, *mental* and *medical* are not synonymous. One refers to the mind, the other to the body.

Psychological counseling does not deal with the physical brain. It deals with aspects of thinking, feeling, and behaving. Therefore, the psychotherapist is not in the business of healing diseases, but of teaching new ways of thinking, feeling, and behaving. He is a teacher, not a doctor.

Many have dishonestly used the term *mental illness* to describe a whole host of problems of thinking and behaving which should be labeled as "problems of living." Though the term *mental illness* is a misnomer and a mismatch of words, it has become firmly ingrained in the public vocabulary and is glibly pronounced on all sorts of occasions by both lay and professional persons. Jonas Robitscher says:

> Our culture is permeated with psychiatric thought. Psychiatry, which had its beginnings in the care of the sick, has expanded its net to include everyone, and it exercises its authority over this total population by methods that range from enforced therapy and coerced control to the advancement of ideas and the promulgation of values.

A Way to Avoid Responsibility for Behavior

The very term *mental illness* has become a blight on society. If we really believe that a person with a mental-emotional-behavioral problem is sick, then we have admitted that he is no longer responsible for his behavior. And if he is not responsible for his behavior, who is?

Mental Illness Is a Myth

If "mental illness" is really a brain disease, it would be listed as such in standard textbooks on pathology. It is not listed as a brain disease because it does not meet the nosological criteria for disease classification. . . . Mental illness is a metaphorical disease, not a literal one. It can no more be "treated" than can a "sick" joke. . . .

Since there are no objective tests for "mental illness," all kinds of socially unacceptable behaviors will be declared "mental illnesses." This gives families a guilt-free opportunity to get rid of disturbing relatives in the name of compassion. It gives mental-health professionals a money-making opportunity to peddle their wares in the name of "treatment." And it gives social parasites and predators an opportunity to avoid responsibility for their behaviors. . . .

The bottom line is this: Behaviors cannot be diseases. Mental illness is a contradiction in terms. Mental illness is a myth.

Jeffrey A. Schaler, *Philadelphia Inquirer*, August 22, 1998.

The psychoanalytic and behavioristic approaches preach that man's behavior is fixed by forces outside of his control.

In the psychoanalytic approach man is controlled by inner psychic forces; in the behavioristic approach man is controlled by outer environmental forces. If man's behavior is determined by internal or external uncontrollable forces, it follows that he is not responsible for his behavior. Thus criminals are allowed to plea bargain on the basis of "temporary insanity," "diminished capacity," and "incompetent to stand trial." The full impact on the evils unleashed upon society by the psychoanalytical professionals is yet to be realized.

Few Available to Help

Meanwhile, the mystique surrounding the term *mental illness* has frightened away people who could be of great help to those suffering from problems of living. Many people who want to help individuals with problems of living feel "unqualified" to help a person labeled "mentally ill." The confusion inherent within this strange juxtaposition of terms has led to errors which have often been more harmful than helpful to those thus labeled.

Case histories abound of governmental intrusion into personal lives, forced incarceration in mental institutions, deprivation of personal rights, and loss of livelihoods because of the stigma attached to the term "mental illness." Nevertheless, the profession continues to promote the false concept of mental illness, to align it with medicine, and consign it to science—and the public follows. Worse yet, the Church follows.

> "*Neurologists and biopsychiatrists are now finding that the normal problems of normal people are gray and silver shadow versions of full-color mental illness.*"

Some Unusual Behaviors Are Signs of Mental Illness

John Ratey and Catherine Johnson

John Ratey and Catherine Johnson assert in the following viewpoint that many people experience "normal craziness" that manifests itself as compulsive or eccentric behavior. Ratey and Johnson contend that "normal craziness" is actually mild versions of mental illness, and therefore the extent of mental illness is underdiagnosed. The authors maintain that "normal craziness" is due to biological disturbances in the brain; therefore, Ratey and Johnson argue, it can be treated once it is diagnosed. Ratey is an assistant professor of psychiatry at Harvard Medical School and executive director of research at Medfield State Hospital in Massachusetts. Johnson is a trustee of the National Alliance for Autism Research. They are coauthors of *Shadow Syndromes*.

As you read, consider the following questions:
1. According to the authors, what factors influence "normal craziness?"
2. How does life change when people accept the fact that they have hidden or partial mental disorders, in the authors' view?
3. In the authors' opinion, how do researchers know that mental white noise is biologically based?

Although the face Sandra presents to others is that of a relaxed and loyal friend, internally she is never at ease—she is driven to clean the house obsessively, or diet obsessively, or, most recently, to shop obsessively, having run up a debt of $15,000 within a few years' time. We might guess that Sandra comes from a dysfunctional family. Perhaps her parents were too demanding, or drank too much, or inflicted upon her their bad habits and character flaws. But neither we nor Sandra might suspect that there might be something biological going on.

Or take the case of Lou, a man who continually scans his body for signs of trouble, despite being in excellent condition for a man of 50. Lou not only worries obsessively about minor physical ailments, but compulsively questions his physician-wife about whether any of these troubles might be cancer. How do we explain Lou's behavior? Perhaps we see it as "normal craziness" similar to the obsessive neatness of the main character Jerry on the television show *Seinfeld*. Maybe we also view Lou as the victim of a bad childhood. What we don't think is that Lou, like Sandra, might be at the mercy of his own flawed brain chemistry.

Shadow Syndromes

But neuropsychiatry is now discovering that a great deal of "normal craziness" in fact is heavily influenced by the genetics, structure, and neurochemistry of the brain. Every troublesome personality likely has its roots in an unsuspected brain difference: the loner, the gifted person who cannot seem to live up to his or her potential, the needy neighbor you can't get off the telephone, the confirmed bachelor, the man who cannot talk about his feelings, or even the husband who throws tantrums like a four year old. Neurologists and biopsychiatrists are now finding that the normal problems of normal people are gray and silver shadow versions of full-color mental illnesses. They're the same thing in outline, but indistinct in detail, and not easy to recognize for what they are. Just as shadows cast a pall across a day that might otherwise be sunny and clear, these "shadow syndromes" cast a shadow over the realms of work and love.

Life changes when we begin to realize that people can

have subtle, hidden, or partial mental disorders. The impulse to blame people or their parents for their problems loses its power. The profound and corrosive sense of shame we feel over our own behavior begins to lift when we understand that it can be created by subtle differences in the brain. And the notion of the shadow syndrome helps us to see that talk therapy needs to address our biological selves as well as our psychological selves. Sandra, for example, sought out therapists and doctors to help her change her behaviors, but they focused on the fact that she was adopted—a fact that she had thought little about. However her childhood may be affecting her, Sandra faces challenges shaped by the facts of her biology as well, and she needs the help of her therapists in doing so.

This is not to dismiss our environments as a major source of who and what we are. A child with an innately anxious temperament who is born to an innately anxious mother may grow up to be a different person from the child with the anxious temperament whose mother does not share his difficulty. But the "new" biology can help us understand how environment and biology work together to create the person—an understanding that we can use to make the changes we wish and hope to make.

Diagnosing Shadows

In order to understand "normal craziness," we can learn from "craziness" that is not so normal, such as schizophrenia or severe manic depression. Psychiatrists diagnose their patients with these and other disorders according to syndromes described in *DSM-IV*, the *Diagnostic and Statistical Manual, Fourth Edition*. A syndrome is a set of behaviors that consistently appear together, and which the patient, the doctor, or the patient's friends and family can observe and describe. However, real people often come into the doctor's office exhibiting only one or two symptoms of a particular syndrome, or may fit every aspect of a syndrome down to the smallest detail and yet be so mildly affected that even a good therapist might miss the diagnosis. In fact, most everyday people seem to have minor bits of this syndrome, small pieces of that.

Lou's hypochondriacal behavior can be seen as a mild version of obsessive-compulsive disorder (OCD), and Sandra has shown "streaks" of the syndromes on the anxiety spectrum. Other common shadow syndromes are mild but hidden depression; hypomania, a mildly manic state where a person possesses extraordinary energy and productivity and lacks ordinary self-doubt; mild rage problems, such as that of the tantruming husband; mild attention deficit disorder (ADD), which does not unravel a life but may leave it disorganized; and autism-like social deficits that make a person incapable of relating well to others.

Mental Illness in America

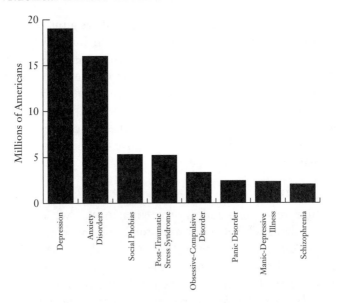

National Institute of Mental Health, *The Numbers Count*, 1999.

One of the most confusing issues is how many of the shadow syndromes normal people may fit. Sometimes depressed, sometimes impulsive, sometimes manic, sometimes obsessed: we may find aspects of ourselves, our families, and our friends in all of these categories. But there is one characteristic every shadow syndrome has in common: mental white noise. When we are mildly depressed, or mildly hyperactive, or mildly anything else, our brains cease to function as the quiet, reflective center of an ordered world. We become noisy on the inside.

What stress is to the body, noise is to the brain: the general response to the demands made upon it by difficult life circumstances or by flawed biology. The noisy brain cannot separate out stimuli or thoughts, either incoming or outgoing. For example, a person with mild ADD cannot filter stimuli from the environment; he or she will see everything out there, all at once.

A noisy brain invariably affects a person's capacity to deal with other people. Social skills occupy the very topmost level of the brain. Noise affects this top level, or cortex, causing the person afflicted to fall back to a more primitive, "lower" level of brain functioning that corresponds to the social strategies of the adolescent or child—or lower still, to the level of the "reptilian brain," where we respond reflexively instead of thoughtfully.

Brain-Based Behavior

How do we know that this mental white noise is biologically based? In the case of obsessive-compulsive disorder, researchers have identified three specific brain structures that become locked together in a pattern and cause the behavior. Any damage to the primary brain structure, the caudate nucleus, whether from "bad genes," head injury, or even from the body's own immune system, can result in obsessive-compulsive disorder. In fact, OCD can develop in children as a result of a strep throat infection. The same antibody that attacks strep can also attack the caudate nucleus, causing a child to develop obsessive fears of contamination and to begin compulsively hand-washing. Treatment with blood plasma and antibiotics makes these symptoms decline noticeably.

But unlike obsessive-compulsive disorder, other shadow syndromes such as adult tantruming do not have their roots in a simple biological problem. In fact, many readers will be skeptical as to whether adult tantruming has a biological explanation at all. And yet antidepressant medications have been shown to stop anger attacks altogether in 71 percent of a group of depressed patients, and reduce their incidence in the rest. This fact alone implies that for these patients, tantrums had a significant brain-based component.

It is also likely that temper tantrums in people who are not depressed are just as biologically based as anger attacks in depressed people. The experience of Gary, a man who averaged forty tantrums a month, provides evidence for this conclusion. By the time he went to see a psychiatrist, Gary had exhausted almost every available avenue to master his temper, except for medication. He had been a sober member of Alcoholics Anonymous for 10 years; he regularly attended a men's group to discuss feelings and relationships; he had been a runner for years; he had religiously practiced breathing, meditation, and relaxation exercises to calm himself. And none of it had worked. His second marriage was on the brink of collapse and his small daughter was terrified.

Gary went to see a psychiatrist because he had read about attention deficit disorder, and recognized symptoms in himself. The psychiatrist confirmed Gary's self-diagnosis, and prescribed a low dosage of the medication desipramine as treatment. Later, Gary self-consciously revealed a side-benefit from the medication: He had stopped having tantrums at home.

The fact that desipramine worked so well for Gary indicates that his tantrums very likely were the result of brain noise produced by random firings of the brain stem. An excess of mental noise from this lower region, which connects the brain with the spinal cord, can overwhelm the higher brain centers, the "seat of reason" found in the frontal lobes of the cortex, and allow the lower emotional brain to take over. In other words, emotion "hijacks" reason. Desipramine may act to reduce random, noisy brain-stem firings. By quieting these posterior areas, desipramine may then permit the frontal lobes to step in and stave off a rage attack.

A Wholesome Solution

Gary's experience shows how a person can go about changing the way his or her brain works. First, the person must try to develop insight—to see himself as his loved ones see him. The person also needs to consult a doctor, and listen to what that doctor tells him or her about brain chemistry. Then, working with the doctor and loved ones, the person needs to create tools to short-circuit his or her biologically based response to daily life. Finally, if these measures are not sufficient, he or she may have to take medication to restore brain functioning.

While relaxation exercises had not worked for Gary's rage attacks, insight and behavioral techniques alone have helped many people with shadow syndromes change. In a revolutionary UCLA study, obsessive-compulsive patients—those suffering from symptoms more severe than Sandra's or Lou's—were required to tell themselves that the obsession they were experiencing was not real. Then they resisted performing the compulsion and instead forced themselves to do something wholesome and enjoyable—such as a hobby, volunteer work, or a good deed for a friend or a loved one—for at least 15 minutes. Twelve out of 18 patients in the study experienced striking reductions in their obsessive-compulsive symptoms. And, remarkably, the changes were reflected in before-and-after brain scans. In the "after" scans, several brain areas had begun to operate as they do in the normal brain. The UCLA researchers demonstrated the power of the mind to bend a malfunctioning brain to its will. . . .

The Wings of Change

Perhaps the most useful theorem for anyone trying to change his brain is meteorologist Edward Lorenz's now famous "butterfly effect": a butterfly flapping its wings in Tokyo, he imagined, could set off a cascading chain of events that ended up as a hurricane over Texas. This theorem applies to mental fitness as well. The brain's interconnectivity tells us that small problems may cascade into large ones, so it can be important not to let even minor mental issues slide.

However, the good news is that complex systems such as the brain do not list in just one direction: Life is not inevitably a downhill proposition. A change as small as a new exercise program or a satisfying hobby might make all the difference in the world.

For most of us, the notion that a complex system may tip up as well as down is counterintuitive. As a culture, we have taken the second law of thermodynamics to heart: entropy rules. But we do possess some intuitive understanding of an anti-entropy force at work in life and love, when we speak of "things falling into place," or of being "on a roll," or when athletes hit "a winning streak." All of these experiences are, in a sense, what we are hoping for when we think of changing our lives. We are hoping to reach that magic moment when life and love "self organize" into something splendid.

With greater knowledge of the brain's biology, people who struggle with shadow syndromes can move closer to that goal. We hope that the shame of having to live life as a flawed human being will eventually fade, and the potential to free the self from the bonds of biology will grow strong. We hope that it will help people to begin the journey out from the shadows and into the clear light of day.

"The 'bible' of mental health professionals classifies many kinds of traditionally feminine behavior as signs of mental disorder but has no category that pathologizes unhealthy, traditionally masculine behavior."

Normal Women's Behavior Is Erroneously Classified as Mental Illness

Paula J. Caplan

Paula J. Caplan argues in the following viewpoint that many of the mental health professionals who consulted in the compilation of mental disorders in the *Diagnostic and Statistical Manual of Mental Disorders* (DSM) are misogynistic white males who pathologized normal female behavior. Furthermore, the American Psychiatric Association is chauvinistic in that it refuses to recognize unhealthy, traditionally masculine behavior as mental disorders. Caplan, a clinical and research psychologist, is the author of *They Say You're Crazy: How the World's Most Powerful Psychiatrists Decide Who's Normal.*

As you read, consider the following questions:
1. According to Caplan, why is the *Diagnostic and Statistical Manual of Mental Disorders* so influential?
2. What are two of the misogynist diagnoses in the DSM, as cited by the author?
3. What is the real cause of women's suffering, according to Caplan?

Excerpted from "Talking Feminist," by Paula J. Caplan, *On the Issues*, Winter 1997. Reprinted with the permission of Paula J. Caplan.

When sociologist Margrit Eichler and I first composed our made-up mental disorder, "Delusional Dominating Personality Disorder (DDPD)," to classify traditionally sexist men's behavior as a mental illness, it was a consciousness-raising and educational exercise. Whenever we would read the DDPD criteria to groups of students or other audiences (see "Do You Recognize This Man?"), they would invariably begin by laughing when they heard the first few. By the middle questions, they'd be listening intently, and, by the last ones, they were yelling out, "This is a real problem! I know people like this!"

Trying to Classify DDPD as a Mental Disorder

Eventually, we came to the conclusion that it should be more than an exercise. So in 1989, we asked the American Psychiatric Association (APA) to add DDPD to its list of official mental illnesses. After all, its diagnostic handbook—*The Diagnostic and Statistical Manual of Mental Disorders* (DSM), the "bible" of mental health professionals—classifies many kinds of traditionally feminine behavior as signs of mental disorder but has no category that pathologizes unhealthy, traditionally masculine behavior. There is no "John Wayne syndrome" or "macho personality disorder." In our proposal to the APA, we pointed out that DDPD gave the organization the opportunity to take a leadership role in recognizing this cluster of behavior as a significant social problem. We also noted that some women, as well as some men, fit the DDPD symptom picture and that it often characterizes military and political leaders and the heads of major corporations.

When I told Margrit that I didn't care much for the term "mental disorder" and suspected there wasn't a chance that DDPD would get into the DSM, she replied, "We submit it, and we save the correspondence."

Was she ever right. The letters the DSM leaders sent and the material in the minutes of their meetings revealed the process by which this powerful handful of people decides who is normal and which diagnoses are admitted or kept out of their "bible." Understanding this process is important because the DSM, now in its fourth edition, is so influential. Its previous edition sold over a million copies, earned more than a million dollars for the APA, and was translated into 17 languages. Virtually all psychotherapy patients whose insurance pays for their therapy receive a DSM label that goes into their file and is sent to the insurers.

Although the APA is quite reluctant to look at new ways of diagnosing problems mainly associated with white males—no doubt at least partly because the gatekeepers of the DSM are a handful of mostly white, mostly male American psychiatrists and a few psychologists—it has been very open to adding categories that pathologize women. A brief look at a tiny fraction of these misogynist diagnoses reveals some of the dangers that await any woman:

Premenstrual syndrome was classified as a severe mental illness affecting at least half a million American women as of the 1987 DSM edition. This is not about chocolate cravings and uterine cramps or even some irritability or depression (men have been proved to be more irritable than premenstrual women, and researchers' efforts to find more depression premenstrually than at other times have failed). It is about claiming that 500,000 women in this country are mentally disordered in some presumably female-hormone—related way, despite evidence that is not the case.

An Attempt to Control Women

As I learned when I served on two DSM committees (before resigning because I was appalled by the process), the people who ultimately make the decisions about what goes into the book and what is kept out are willing to ignore and distort research, even invent diagnostic categories. Despite the APA's own literature review, which yielded little information about whether a premenstrual mental disorder existed and revealed that the little available research was very "preliminary" and plagued by many methodological problems, the committee on this topic recommended that the category go into the next edition of the manual, and indeed it did. It is there now.

The practice of calling women who are suffering "masochists" and attributing their suffering to a conscious or unconscious "need to suffer" has not abated since Freud's disciple Helena Deutsch named masochism as one of femininity's three essential features (along with passivity and narcissism).

The myth that women are masochists is regularly used to justify ignoring the real causes of women's suffering, such as oppression and violence. Even Gloria Steinem, in an otherwise

Do You Recognize This Man?*

A quiz you'll never see in *Cosmo* and *Redbook*

Men who meet at least six of the following criteria may have Delusional Dominating Personality Disorder! Warning: DDPD is pervasive, profound, and a maladaptive organization of the entire personality! (Check as many as apply.)

1. Is he . . .

- unable to establish and maintain meaningful interpersonal relationships?
- unable to identify and express a range of feelings in himself (typically accompanied by an inability to identify accurately the feelings of other people)?
- unable to respond appropriately and empathically to the feelings and needs of close associates and intimates (often leading to the misinterpretation of signals from others)?
- unable to derive pleasure from doing things for others?

2. Does he . . .

- use power, silence, withdrawal, and/or avoidance rather than negotiation in the face of interpersonal conflict or difficulty?
- believe that women are responsible for the bad things that happen to him, while the good things are due to his own abilities, achievements, or efforts?
- inflate the importance and achievements of himself, males in general, or both?
- categorize spheres of functioning and sets of behavior rigidly according to sex (like believing housework is women's work)?
- use a gender-based double standard in interpreting or evaluating situations or behavior (considering a man who makes breakfast sometimes to be extraordinarily good, for example, but considering a woman who sometimes neglects to make breakfast deficient)?
- feel inordinately threatened by women who fail to disguise their intelligence?
- display any of the following delusions:
  - the delusion that men are entitled to the services of any woman with whom they are personally associated;

brilliant critique of Freud's work (based on the premise "If Freud had been a woman") neglects to question that aspect of his theory. And Steinem has repeatedly said for publication

- – the delusion that women like to suffer and be ordered around;
- – the delusion that physical force is the best method of solving interpersonal problems;
- – the delusion that men's sexual and aggressive impulses are uncontrollable;
- – the delusion that pornography and erotica are identical;
- – the delusion that women control most of the world's wealth and/or power but do little of the world's work;
- – the delusion that existing inequalities in the distribution of power and wealth are a product of the survival of the fittest and that, therefore, allocation of greater social and economic rewards to the already privileged are merited.

3. Does he have . . .

• a pathological need to affirm his social importance by displaying himself in the company of females who meet any three of these criteria:
  - – are conventionally physically attractive; or
  - – are younger;
  - – are shorter;
  - – weigh less;
  - – appear to be lower on socioeconomic criteria; *or*
  - – are more submissive . . . than he is?

• a distorted approach to sexuality, displaying itself in one or both of these ways:
  - – a pathological need for flattery about his sexual performance and/or the size of his genitalia;
  - – an infantile tendency to equate large breasts on women with their sexual attractiveness.

• emotionally uncontrolled resistance to reform efforts that are oriented toward gender equity?

The tendency to consider himself a "New Man" neither proves nor disproves that the subject fits within this diagnostic category.

Some women also fit many of these criteria, either because they wish to be as dominant as men or because they feel men should be dominant.

Paula J. Caplan, *On the Issues*, Winter 1997.

that "any woman who is not a feminist is a masochist," a remark that implies that some women do like to suffer.

Then there's "Munchausen's syndrome by proxy." In child-custody disputes, when mothers allege that their ex-husbands have sexually abused their children, lawyers representing fathers are quick to find therapists who will diagnose these mothers as having the proxy version of this syndrome. Munchausen's syndrome has long been used to describe people—often, women—who are said to go from doctor to doctor, supposedly seeking one who will tell them that something is terribly wrong with them physically and will perform surgery on them. The "proxy" form of the syndrome is said to apply to a person with a sick need to believe that something terrible is happening to her child. These cases do exist, but they're very rare. More commonly, Munchausen's syndrome by proxy is a fancy way of saying that it's not the abusive father but rather the mother who reports the abuse who should be pathologized, condemned, and disbelieved.

Of all of the misogynist mechanisms feminists have uncovered in the past century, one of the most insidious has been the diagnosing of women as mentally ill in order to maintain control over individual women and women as a group. Psychologist Phyllis Chesler's brilliant book *Women and Madness* remains the classic in the field. Although it was first published in 1972, it is still eerily up-to-date.

Women as Scapegoats

We have to protest the use and misuse of diagnosis to keep women down. The dangers are great for white, heterosexual, able-bodied women in middle adulthood. They are even greater for women who do not fit those categories. (Therapists have been shown to be more inclined to pathologize such women than to pathologize either white, heterosexual, able-bodied women or men.)

Societies tend to have scapegoats, whom they use to keep power for themselves in the following way: If anyone complains about the status quo, those in power lay the blame on the scapegoats, as in "It's these feminists who insist on having careers who are responsible for the high rate of unemployment, juvenile crime, and men's impotence." Thus, women who silently endure abuse can be diagnosed as masochistic or "self-defeating"; women who try to protect their children from abusive ex-husbands can be diagnosed as suffering from "Munchausen's by proxy"; and those who respond to oppression or control with irritability and anger can be diagnosed as having "premenstrual dysphoric disorder," as it's called in the DSM.

In North America, we are inclined to believe that mental health is an arena in which other people are the experts, that there is some Real Truth about who is mentally ill, that we probably don't even know the right questions to ask and would make fools of ourselves if we protested. But when being labeled as mentally disordered can deprive us of custody of our children, of possibilities for employment and for disability and health insurance, and of the legal right to make decisions about our lives, there is too much at stake for us to agree to let these fears strangle our speech.

"We have neglected morality and turned our culture into a nonjudgmental support group."

Immoral Behavior Should Not Be Excused as a Sign of Mental Illness

Dennis Prager

American society is too quick to forgive evil behavior by linking it to mental illness, Dennis Prager maintains in the following viewpoint. He cites the case of Larry Froistad, who confessed to an on-line support group that he murdered his daughter. Prager notes that many people in the group expressed support for Froistad and stated concern over his mental health. According to Prager, such a response shows how Americans have become too nonjudgmental and are not willing to condemn immoral behavior. Prager is a radio talk-show host.

As you read, consider the following questions:
1. In the author's opinion, when did America become "a big support group"?
2. What is one of the characteristics of violent criminals, according to Prager?
3. Who is condemned in modern society, in Prager's opinion?

The details of the alleged crime were gruesome enough: Larry Froistad, 29, confessed to his on-line alcoholism support group that he had murdered his five-year-old daughter, Amanda, in 1995 during a custody battle with his ex-wife. According to the *New York Times*, Mr. Froistad set his house on fire with Amanda inside, climbed out the window, and then, in Mr. Froistad's words, "set about putting on a show of shock, surprise and grief to remove culpability from myself. Dammit, part of that show was climbing in her window and . . . hearing her breathe and dropping her where she was so she could die and rid me of her mother's interferences."

If anything could be more horrifying than this, it is the reaction of some fellow members of the support group, Moderation Management. While several reported the confession to authorities, others opposed informing and expressed support for Mr. Froistad. One member, for example, expressed concern that Mr. Froistad "might be contemplating suicide" over "what seems to have become for you an awful situation." He urged Mr. Froistad "to seriously think about contacting a therapist and working things through with yourself in a safe manner."

Another user sent an angry e-mail to a man who had informed the authorities: "Just how big a pervert are you? I bet you really get off talking to the FBI. Wow. Did you ask them if you could see their guns?" (Mr. Froistad has been charged with murder; his lawyers have indicated he is "mentally ill" and will plead not guilty.) [Froistad later pled guilty and was sentenced to forty years in prison.]

The reaction of Mr. Froistad's support group provides a microcosm—and an explanation—for much of America's moral confusion. Since the 1960s, America has become a big support group. We are expected to support our fellow citizens, however antisocial they are, and not to judge them. Deviance has been defined down, in Daniel Patrick Moynihan's memorable phrase; and when deviants "open up," they are cheered, as on some television talk shows. This world view can be summed up in a few basic principles:

• *Psychological explanations trump moral standards.* Since the 1960s, the words "good" and "evil" have been largely expunged from the vocabulary of sophisticated Americans.

They speak instead in terms of "healthy" and "sick." That is why we are expected to feel sympathy for people who commit evil acts—after all, they're not responsible for their sickness. Even the Soviet Union, in this view, was a sick empire rather than an evil one: When Moscow shot down a Korean passenger plane in 1983, a psychologist writing in *Psychology Today* warned against labeling it an act of "aggression." Rather, it was an act of "paranoia."

• *Feelings matter more than behavior.* One day when my older son was two years old and playing in a park, a five-year-old boy walked over to him and threw him onto the concrete. The boy's mother, seeing what her son had done, ran over to him and cried, "Honey, what's troubling you?" I knew nothing about this woman, but I was certain that she was highly educated. One must *learn* to respond the way she did. The average mother a generation ago would have severely reprimanded any child of hers who threw down a toddler.

A Pharmaceutical Excuse

Is anyone so ignorant that he hasn't heard about inappropriate serotonin levels in the brain, and of the wonders of Prozac? Young people who haven't a clue when World War II took place or who fought it are perfectly *au fait* with neurochemistry. They know they would stop shoplifting or mugging if only someone would balance their brain amines for them. Alas, none of the drugs available have done it yet for them. The pharmaceutical companies really ought to try harder, and until they succeed, we must expect to be attacked in the street, to have our houses broken into and our cars stolen.

Theodore Dalrymple, *Wall Street Journal*, April 23, 1998.

• *Self-esteem is more important than self-control.* This shift in emphasis from character to psyche is not only morally wrong but foolish. The belief is that children with high self-esteem will act more responsibly. This is demonstrably false. One of the best scholarly studies of altruism, "The Altruistic Personality," by Sam and Pearl Oliner, is the product of a lifelong study of non-Jewish rescuers of Jews during the Holocaust. Among the conclusions they reached was that there was absolutely no correlation between self-esteem and the likelihood of being a rescuer or a Nazi murderer.

Going even further is Case Western Reserve social psychologist Roy Baumeister in his recent book "Evil." Prof. Baumeister has devoted his career to studying violent criminals, especially murderers. He lists four "root characteristics" of most violent criminals—one of which is *high* self-esteem.

• *Those who condemn evil, not those who commit it, deserve opprobrium.* As David Gelernter notes in his book "Drawing Life: Surviving the Unabomber," the pejorative term "judgmental" didn't even appear in the dictionary before about 1970. People took it for granted that it was the duty of moral individuals to make moral judgments. In our new age, those who judge evil behavior—who value morality more than psychology—must be condemned.

Psychology has important insights to offer, and psychotherapy can be immensely valuable—as can support groups based on moral values, such as Alcoholics Anonymous. But having imbibed too much from the heady waters of psychology, we have neglected morality and turned our culture into a nonjudgmental support group. Larry Froistad's case is atypical only because it is so extreme.

Periodical Bibliography

The following articles have been selected to supplement the diverse views presented in this chapter. Addresses are provided for periodicals not indexed in the *Readers' Guide to Periodical Literature*, the *Alternative Press Index*, the *Social Sciences Index*, or the *Index to Legal Periodicals and Books*.

Jerry Adler	"My Brain Made Me Do It," *Newsweek*, January 26, 1998.
Sharon Begley	"Is Everybody Crazy?" *Newsweek*, January 26, 1998.
Jane E. Brody	"Many Smokers Who Can't Quit Are Mentally Ill, a Study Finds," *New York Times*, August 27, 1997.
Jane E. Brody	"Study Challenges Idea of PMS as Emotional Disorder," *New York Times*, January 22, 1998.
Michelle Cottle	"Selling Shyness," *New Republic*, August 2, 1999.
Donna Foote and Sam Seibert	"The Age of Anxiety," *Newsweek*, Spring/Summer 1999.
Kay Redfield Jamison	"A World Apart," *Newsweek*, Spring/Summer 1999.
Susana McCollom	"Reincarnating Freud," *Z Magazine*, March 1997.
Margie Patlak	"Schizophrenia: Real Lives Ravaged by Imaginary Terror," *FDA Consumer*, September/October 1997.
Phnom Penh Post	"A Legacy of Mental Ills," *World Press Review*, June 1999.
Joe Sharkey	"Paranoia Is Universal. Its Symptoms Are Not," *New York Times*, August 2, 1998.
Kelly Starling	"Black Women and the Blues," *Ebony*, May 1999.
Thomas Szasz	"Gullible Skeptics," *Freeman*, May 1999. Available from 30 S. Broadway, Irvington-on-Hudson, NY 10533.
Thomas Szasz	"Mental Illness Is Still a Myth," *Society*, May/June 1994.
James Trilling	"My Father and the Weak-Eyed Devils," *American Scholar*, Spring 1999.

CHAPTER 2

How Should Society Deal with the Mentally Ill?

Chapter Preface

One controversial element of society's attitude toward the mentally ill is the insanity defense—the argument that a person accused of a crime is not guilty because, due to mental illness, he cannot control his actions or understand the difference between right and wrong. Although this defense is used in only one percent of criminal cases and successful in only one-quarter of those, opposition to the "not guilty by reason of insanity" verdict has led thirteen states to permit a verdict of "guilty but mentally ill." Defendants convicted under that verdict are held responsible for their crimes but may be provided mental health care in a prison or hospital.

Supporters of "guilty but mentally ill" argue that this verdict, in addition to acknowledging the defendant's responsibility, protects society because it ensures that mentally ill offenders will remain incarcerated and not be released from a mental institution prematurely. Richard E. Vatz and Lee S. Weinberg, associate psychology editors for *USA Today* magazine, further contend that "guilty but mentally ill" shows greater respect for victims and their families. They write: "Such a verdict may lessen the terrible suffering experienced by victims' families by acknowledging that the perpetrators must be punished."

Critics of "guilty but mentally ill" argue that the verdict is flawed, in part because those who are convicted do not necessarily receive psychiatric treatment. A 1996 article in the *Detroit News* stated that only 41 of the 308 inmates in Michigan prisons who were judged "guilty but mentally ill" were receiving in-patient care. The remaining inmates received little or no mental health treatment. The American Psychiatric Association also criticizes the verdict, claiming that its use absolves the legal system from the obligation of "deciding, through its deliberations, how society defines responsibility."

The treatment of the mentally ill under the criminal justice system is only one issue that society must consider. Most mentally ill persons are not criminals and so questions such as how they ought to be treated in public and in the workplace must also be evaluated. In the following chapter, the authors debate how society should deal with the mentally ill.

"Deinstitutionalization has helped create the mental illness crisis."

Severely Mentally Ill Persons Should Be Institutionalized

E. Fuller Torrey

In the following viewpoint, E. Fuller Torrey asserts that de-institutionalization—taking severely mentally ill people out of public institutions and closing all or some of those institutions—has worsened the mental health crisis. He contends that while some people with severe mental illnesses have benefited from deinstitutionalization, many others need to remain in institutions. He argues that the closings have harmed a significant minority of the mentally ill by making it difficult for them to receive necessary treatment. Torrey is the author of *Out of the Shadows: Confronting America's Mental Illness Crisis*, from which this viewpoint is taken.

As you read, consider the following questions:

1. According to the author, what event led to deinstitutionalization?
2. In 1994, how many severely mentally ill patients were in public psychiatric hospitals in the United States, according to Torrey?
3. How does Torrey define "self-determination" for the people harmed by deinstitutionalization?

The mental illness crisis . . . consists of hundreds of thousands of men and women . . . who represent a large percentage of the estimated 2.2 million Americans with untreated severe mental illnesses. On any given day, approximately 150,000 of them are homeless, living on the streets or in public shelters. Another 159,000 are incarcerated in jails and prisons, mostly for crimes committed because they were not being treated. Some of them become violent and may terrorize their families, towns, or urban neighborhoods. A very large number have died prematurely as a result of accidents and suicide. Tragically, most of these instances of homelessness, incarcerations, episodes of violence, and premature deaths are unnecessary. We know what to do, but for economic, legal, and ideological reasons we fail to do it. . . .

The Magnitude of Deinstitutionalization

Deinstitutionalization is the name given to the policy of moving severely mentally ill people out of large state institutions and then closing part or all of those institutions; it has been a major contributing factor to the mental illness crisis. (The term also describes a similar process for mentally retarded people, but the focus of this viewpoint is exclusively on severe mental illnesses.)

Deinstitutionalization began in 1955 with the widespread introduction of chlorpromazine, commonly known as Thorazine, the first effective antipsychotic medication, and received a major impetus 10 years later with the enactment of federal Medicaid and Medicare. Deinstitutionalization has two parts: the moving of the severely mentally ill out of the state institutions, and the closing of part or all of those institutions. The former affects people who are already mentally ill. The latter affects those who become ill after the policy has gone into effect and for the indefinite future because hospital beds have been permanently eliminated.

The magnitude of deinstitutionalization of the severely mentally ill qualifies it as one of the largest social experiments in American history. In 1955, there were 558,239 severely mentally ill patients in the nation's public psychiatric hospitals. In 1994, this number had been reduced by 486,620 patients, to 71,619, as seen in Figure 1. It is important to note, however, that the census of 558,239 patients in public psychiatric hospitals in 1955 was in relationship to the nation's total population at the time, which was 164 million.

By 1994, the nation's population had increased to 260 million. If there had been the same proportion of patients per population in public mental hospitals in 1994 as there had been in 1955, the patients would have totaled 885,010. The true magnitude of deinstitutionalization, then, is the difference between 885,010 and 71,619. In effect, approximately 92 percent of the people who would have been living in public psychiatric hospitals in 1955 were not living there in 1994. Even allowing for the approximately 40,000 patients who occupied psychiatric beds in general hospitals or the approximately 10,000 patients who occupied psychiatric beds in community mental health centers (CMHCs) on any given day in 1994, that still means that approximately 763,391 severely mentally ill people (over three-quarters of a million) are living in the community today who would have been hospitalized 40 years ago. That number is more than the population of Baltimore or San Francisco.

Varying Results

Deinstitutionalization varied from state to state. In assessing these differences in census for public mental hospitals, it is not sufficient merely to subtract the 1994 number of patients from the 1955 number, because state populations shifted in the various states during those 40 years. In Iowa, West Virginia, and the District of Columbia, the total populations actually decreased during that period, whereas in California, Florida, and Arizona, the population increased dramatically; and in Nevada, it increased more than sevenfold, from 0.2 million to 1.5 million. . . .

Rhode Island, Massachusetts, New Hampshire, Vermont, West Virginia, Arkansas, Wisconsin, and California all have effective deinstitutionalization rates of over 95 percent. Rhode Island's rate is over 98 percent, meaning that for every 100 state residents in public mental hospitals in 1955, fewer than 2 patients are there today. On the other end of the curve, Nevada, Delaware, and the District of Columbia have effective deinstitutionalization rates below 80 percent.

Inadequate Treatment and Understanding

Most of those who were deinstitutionalized from the nation's public psychiatric hospitals were severely mentally ill. Between 50 and 60 percent of them were diagnosed with schizophrenia. Another 10 to 15 percent were diagnosed with manic-depressive illness and severe depression. An additional 10 to 15 percent were diagnosed with organic brain diseases—epilepsy, strokes, Alzheimer's disease, and brain damage secondary to trauma. The remaining individuals residing in public psychiatric hospitals had conditions such as mental retardation with psychosis, autism and other psychiatric disorders of childhood, and alcoholism and drug addiction with concurrent brain damage. The fact that most deinstitutionalized people suffer from various forms of brain

Fewer of the Mentally Ill Are Being Hospitalized

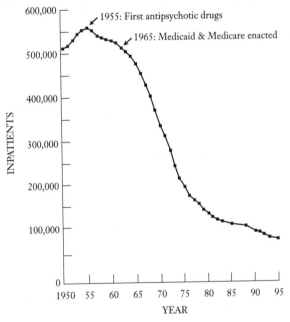

Figure 1. Number of inpatients in public mental hospitals 1950 through 1995.

Source: E. Fuller Torrey, *Out of the Shadows: Confronting America's Mental Illness Crisis*, 1997.

dysfunction was not as well understood when the policy of deinstitutionalization got under way.

Thus deinstitutionalization has helped create the mental illness crisis by discharging people from public psychiatric hospitals without ensuring that they received the medication and rehabilitation services necessary for them to live successfully in the community. Deinstitutionalization further exacerbated the situation because, once the public psychiatric beds had been closed, they were not available for people who later became mentally ill, and this situation continues up to the present. Consequently, approximately 2.2 million severely mentally ill people do not receive any psychiatric treatment.

Deinstitutionalization was based on the principle that severe mental illness should be treated in the least restrictive setting. As further defined by President Jimmy Carter's Commission on Mental Health, this ideology rested on "the objective of maintaining the greatest degree of freedom, self-determination, autonomy, dignity, and integrity of body, mind, and spirit for the individual while he or she participates in treatment or receives services." This is a laudable goal and for many, perhaps for the majority of those who are deinstitutionalized, it has been at least partially realized.

For a substantial minority, however, deinstitutionalization has been a psychiatric *Titanic*. Their lives are virtually devoid of "dignity" or "integrity of body, mind, and spirit." "Self-determination" often means merely that the person has a choice of soup kitchens. The "least restrictive setting" frequently turns out to be a cardboard box, a jail cell, or a terror-filled existence plagued by both real and imaginary enemies.

VIEWPOINT 2

"Institutionalized individuals are completely separated from the mainstream of community life."

Institutionalization Harms Most Mentally Ill Persons

Ira A. Burnim

In the following viewpoint, Ira A. Burnim argues that the mentally ill should not be institutionalized. He contends that institutionalization is harmful because it segregates those individuals from the rest of society and greatly limits their autonomy. According to Burnim, the poor care often found in institutions can cause psychic damage and the loss of social skills. In his view, resources should be redirected toward services that integrate mentally ill persons with the rest of the community. Burnim is a lawyer for the Judge David L. Bazelon Center for Mental Health Law in Washington, D.C.

As you read, consider the following questions:

1. According to Burnim, what are the two conditions that need to be met in order for a state to offer community services?
2. When should the mentally ill be institutionalized, as stated by the author?
3. According to the author, what are some examples of the psychic damage suffered by patients in state hospitals?

Excerpted from "The ADA's 'Integration Mandate' Should Promote Community Services," speech given by Ira A. Burnim, to the U.S. Commission on Civil Rights, November 13, 1998, Washington, D.C. (Endnotes in original have been omitted).

In my [viewpoint], I will speak briefly about the "integration mandate" of the Americans with Disabilities Act (ADA) and its significance for people with mental disabilities. The mandate, codified in the regulations implementing Title II [which prohibits discrimination in public services], provides that:

> A public entity shall administer services, programs, and activities in the most integrated setting appropriate to the needs of qualified individuals with disabilities.

Among other things, this regulation requires states to offer community services to residents of institutions, when certain conditions are met. The conditions are that: (1) the residents could be appropriately served in the community, and (2) to serve the residents in a community setting would not fundamentally alter the state's service system or be an undue burden on the state.

Institutionalization Equals Segregation

Institutionalization is the antithesis of integration. Ending unnecessary segregation in institutions was a central purpose of the ADA. The ADA recognizes that the segregation and isolation of individuals with disabilities is a form of discrimination. Congress specifically found, in the text of the ADA itself, that institutionalization was a "critical area" in which "discrimination against individuals with disabilities persists" and which the ADA was intended to remedy.

Historically, people with mental disabilities have been segregated in institutions because societal prejudices have demanded this result. Justice Thurgood Marshall once described the past discrimination against persons with mental disabilities as a "regime of state-mandated segregation and degradation . . . that in its virulence and bigotry rivaled, and indeed paralleled, the worst excesses of Jim Crow".

Congress enacted the ADA in order to remedy our country's history of rampant discrimination against disabled people. The ADA is intended to be a vehicle for insuring the right of disabled people to live independently and participate fully in society. As explained by the House Judiciary Committee, "the ADA is a comprehensive piece of civil rights legislation which promises a new future: a future of inclusion and integration, and the end of exclusion and segregation."

Institutionalization is an extreme form of segregation. Institutionalized individuals are completely separated from the mainstream of community life and have few, if any, opportunities to interact with nondisabled individuals, other than institutional staff. As U.S. District Judge Myron Thompson recently observed, institutionalized individuals "suffer not only a dramatic loss of physical freedom with . . . severely detailed control and invasive treatment, they also cannot enjoy those mundane, daily pleasures—working, shopping, enjoying the companionship of family and friends, or simply being left alone—the loss of which we on the outside would find to be not only intolerable but a threat to our very sanity."

Individuals with disabilities, family members, and professionals recognize that integrated programs are the preferred setting for nearly all people with mental disabilities. The vast majority agree that most individuals with mental disabilities—even those with severe disabilities and complex needs—can live successfully in community settings. The ARC [formerly Association for Retarded Citizens of the United States], the premiere family organization interested in mental retardation, as well as People First, the national self-advocacy organization for people with mental retardation, have proclaimed that no individual with a mental retardation should have to live in an institution. In the field of mental illness, the great weight of family, consumer, and professional opinion is that individuals with mental illness should be institutionalized only for short periods during acute phases of their illness.

The Negatives of Institutionalization

In institutions, schedules are artificially created and mechanically followed. Residents must eat, sleep and carry out all aspects of their daily lives according to schedules that are based on the institution's needs, and that are established and enforced by facility staff. They cannot choose and prepare their own meals; they cannot relax, go outdoors, or spend their time as they see fit; or take care of their personal needs in private. Confined to the grounds, they have little entertainment and few if any job opportunities. They cannot worship with their neighbors or have an active role in family and community life.

As Alabama advocate Ann Marshall has said,

> Consumers, ex-patients, people with mental illness want the opportunity to regain the part of their lives which mental illness has taken from them. They want services and help near their homes, as do people with other illnesses. They want to go down to the local 7-11 for a cold coke on a hot summer day without being part of a "group outing." They want to walk city streets without an "aide" and be able to talk on the telephone any time of the day or night, not as a "privilege" but for the pleasure of talking with a friend. An institution does not give life to people; it only takes it away.

Moreover, institutions are not safe havens. As litigation has repeatedly shown, residents are often victims of poor care, excessive restraint, and even assault. It is important to remember that institutions are generally not tranquil places where treatment and support is continuously provided by highly skilled practitioners. Locked units in particular are often confusing and dehumanizing environments and, for most of the day, they are tended by line staff who are not professionals. Even in the best of institutions, residents tend to lose social skills, as well as other capacities important for independent living. Individuals in state hospitals often suffer from psychic damage such as [according to Priscilla Ridgway] "apathy, mechanization, dehumanization, loss of initiative, submissiveness, resigned acceptance, psychological damage, estrangement, deviant social values, social isolation, dependency, denial and inability to make decisions." Numerous studies have demonstrated that residents improve their functioning, as well as their "quality of life," when they receive care in the community. Again, from Ann Marshall:

> So many times I heard a person say, "How am I ever going to learn how to be well if I'm never around anyone but sick people?". . . These hospital experiences affect the way you feel about yourself and others and adjusting back to the 'normal' world can be extremely difficult, especially if you go back to a world where you have strained personal relationships, lost employment and no supports to help you adjust to community life again.

Today, thousands of individuals with mental disabilities are needlessly segregated in institutions. In most cases, their treating professionals have recommended that they be served in community settings. They remain confined in state developmental centers and psychiatric hospitals contrary to the best judgment of the states' own professionals.

The Future of Community Services

The ADA offers but a single defense for such conduct. To avoid liability under the ADA, a state must prove, in essence, that it would be "unreasonable" to require that community services be offered to those whom it has needlessly institutionalized, because it would work a "fundamental alteration" in the state's service system or impose an "undue financial burden" on the state.

Few, if any states, can establish this defense. In policy if not practice, states have committed themselves to providing care in the "least restrictive setting." All states operate sys-

---

A Community-Based Mental Health System

1. *Treatment:* Treatment services are both diagnostic and therapeutic. Generally, they are provided by professionals or trained personnel to evaluate the nature and extent of an individual's disability and to provide help with learning about and coping with the disability. Treatment services may be provided by an individual or as part of a team process.

A list of potential treatment services may include: 1) intake screening, comprehensive evaluation/assessment and treatment planning; 2) medication therapy and monitoring; 3) outpatient counseling (individual, family and group counseling); 4) mobile community outreach and treatment; 5) crisis intervention and stabilization; 6) intensive day treatment; 7) assistive technology.

2. *Residential services:* Supportive services can be provided as a complement or as part of a range of housing options. Such services should be flexible, increasing or decreasing in intensity based on the individual's needs. Minor home or environmental modifications or adaptive equipment can be used to improve a person's residence to allow for community living, safety, security and accessibility.

Some residential options include: 1) group homes; 2) independent apartments; 3) family or foster (also known as family care) homes; 4) semi-independent apartments; 5) board and care residences.

---

tems of community-based services, and states now serve the majority of their clients in community settings. Given this state of affairs, no "fundamental alteration" is required in the way states operate their service systems, in order to accommodate the community service needs of those left behind in institutions. At most, states must make adjustments to their systems, by redirecting resources and efforts.

Moreover, such adjustments would not impose an "undue burden" on states. As a rule, community services are less expensive institutional services. In Alabama, for example, where we recently litigated claims for community services, the court found that, by closing one bed in a developmental center (an institution for people with mental retardation), the state could save enough money to fund two community placements. While the disparity between the cost of institutional and community services is not everywhere so great, most

---

3. *Rehabilitation services:* Rehabilitation Services are therapeutic activities designed to improve living skills and to assist the person with a disability in realizing their potential for independence and for useful and productive activity, such as work.

Rehabilitation Services include: 1) day programs; 2) psychosocial rehabilitation; 3) educational services; 4) prevocational services; 5) work adjustment training; 6) supported work and transitional employment programs.

4. *Support Services:* Support services assist the person with a disability in their daily life. They are often used to ensure that people with disabilities can access resources such as entitlement benefits, medical care and related services. These services also can assist a person in developing relationships key to their success and stability in community living. Case management services, in particular, are important in helping to create an integrated set of services from an often otherwise fragmented array of state and local resources. Support Services include: 1) case management; 2) intensive case management; 3) family supports; 4) social clubs; 5) advocacy; 6) personal care/home health aide; 7) homemaker and chore services; 8) peer support/self-help group; 9) respite care.

Amici Curiae Brief of National Mental Health Consumers' Self-Help Clearing House, et al., in *Olmstead v. L.C.*, 1998.

---

states could close all their institutions for people with mental retardation and transfer all the residents to community settings at a modest additional cost. The picture is similar when it comes to services for people with mental illness. It would be cost-effective to provide community services to those improperly relegated to the back wards of state hospitals.

Congress anticipated that accommodating the needs of individuals with disabilities would carry some costs. Congress concluded, however, that while the ADA "might pose difficulties for financially strapped state and local governments, . . . the overall long term benefit to society outweighed the costs." As Senator [Orrin] Hatch recognized, at least in the short run, the ADA would impose a lot of expenses and rightly so. It is time we did these things. It is time that we brought persons with disabilities into full freedom, economic and otherwise, with other citizens in our society.

It is time that we brought people with mental disabilities into the mainstream, including the vulnerable and challenged unnecessarily segregated in institutions. To accomplish this, we need meaningful enforcement of the "integration mandate."

> "*We simply cannot afford to deprive anyone of appropriate care for a mental disorder.*"

Mental Health Should Be Treated on a Par with Physical Health

Lewis L. Judd

Mental illnesses should receive the same amount of health care coverage as physical illnesses, Lewis L. Judd claims in the following viewpoint. He argues that mental illnesses can be treated and prevented but that many people are unable to get the mental health care they need because of inadequate insurance coverage. Judd is the chairman of the psychiatry department at the University of California at San Diego and the former director of the National Institute of Mental Health.

As you read, consider the following questions:

1. According to Judd, what do many health care plans do after a patient is in treatment for a mental health problem?
2. How many American children have a diagnosable mental disorder, as stated by the author?
3. In Judd's opinion, what action taken by President Bill Clinton should be emulated by businesses?

Excerpted from "Treatable, If Only . . . ," by Lewis L. Judd, *The San Diego Union-Tribune*, June 16, 1999. Reprinted with permission from the author.

We are entering an era in which we can effectively treat most mental disorders. Our success rate in treating major depression is better than our success rate treating coronary artery disease. Yet, access to services to diagnose and treat mental illness has gotten worse as businesses, insurance plans and managed care companies have cut benefits in order to cut costs.

It is a tragedy that a country which prides itself on equality for all citizens has created a huge underclass of people who are denied access to care and therefore are relegated to lives of chronic disability simply because they have mental illness. This reality applies to the 50 million people who will experience mental illness each year.

Equal Coverage Is Necessary

Scientific advances have established that mental disorders are just like any other medical condition: if left untreated they are among the most disabling conditions people experience and that these disorders can be accurately diagnosed and as effectively treated as any other medical problem. It was time for national health care policy to catch up with what medical science has known for some time, that mental illnesses need the same, equal full coverage as physical illnesses.

A central component of my leadership role as director of the National Institute of Mental Health was the initiation of the National Mental Health Agenda which placed the achievement of parity for the mental disorders as its primary objective. We attacked misperceptions and mythologies that exist about mental illness, which give rise to the pernicious stigmatization of these disorders and have created a climate for inequity in health care benefits. Many of these same messages were reaffirmed and elaborated upon at the White House Conference on Mental Health, in which I was privileged to participate.

Despite the phenomenal progress we have made in recent decades in understanding and treating mental disorders, and despite the high prevalence of conditions such as depression, bipolar depression, panic disorders, obsessive compulsive disorder and schizophrenia, our ability to help patients is significantly handicapped by the inability of patients to get care. The majority of health plans do severely, and uniquely, limit mental health coverage, and even once a patient is in treatment, rigorous efforts are made to terminate or shorten the treatment or demand significantly higher co-payments.

The Costs of Mental Health Care

The most frequently voiced opposition to parity is that "we cannot afford it." However, there are examples in the private sector that access to quality mental health care ultimately results in cost savings. The fact is that we simply cannot afford to deprive anyone of appropriate care for a mental disorder. Nor in good conscience should we tolerate any barriers to care for those with mental illness.

It is a false economy to think that limiting coverage for treatment of mental illness, and therefore limiting access, ultimately saves money for either plans or employers. The costs to society are well documented in terms of worker absenteeism and turnover, use of other medical services for problems directly related to a mental disorder, and the direct relationship between mental illness and suicide, homelessness and involvement with the criminal justice system (it is estimated that 10 percent of the 2 million Americans incarcerated today have a mental disorder).

A Lack of Coverage Can Be Costly

When we don't pay for mental health services through the health care system, we pay for the lack of these services through higher costs of medical care for physical illnesses, through the welfare system, the criminal justice system, in support to our homeless, in addition to lost productivity in the workplace and losses due to premature death from suicide. The indirect costs to society due to lack of treatment are far greater than the direct costs from treatment.

Rosalynn Carter, *Los Angeles Times*, May 7, 1996.

Yet so many of the problems experienced by these patients are completely preventable with intervention and treatment. And this applies to all age groups.

Almost 14 million of our nation's children have a diagnosable mental disorder, but only one-third receive help for these problems.

Our older citizens often have serious mental health problems along with physical health problems, yet their coverage may not allow their problems to be handled effectively through an integrated approach. Americans between 80 and 84 years of age have the highest suicide rate of any population group, nearly twice the rate of the general population.

President Clinton's Policies

The message from the White House conference leaders—President Bill Clinton, Vice President Al Gore, first lady Hillary Rodham Clinton and conference chair Tipper Gore—was unequivocal, clear and strong; that the time had come in America for our citizens with mental disorders to be treated equitably and fairly in health care coverage.

President Clinton has announced a number of important new federal innovations to address this problem including a national campaign to eliminate the stigmatization of mental illnesses. Most importantly he will require, by executive order, that the federal employee health benefit plans provide full parity for mental health with physical health. This will have a positive impact on the lives of 9 million Americans covered under these plans who will now be assured of leading more productive and healthier lives. This action should set an example for all insurers and businesses to follow.

The renewed commitment to support research and education surrounding mental health issues is also encouraging. This will serve to reinforce the efforts of the mental health community to destigmatize these common disabling disorders, bring scientific fact into the forefront, and encourage consumers to demand access to care and support for themselves and their loved ones.

No one should be prevented from living a healthy, fuller life because he or she cannot get basic treatment for a health condition, whether it's a physical or mental disease.

> *"Parity will lead eventually to increases in employer costs and possible elimination of other benefits in some cases, including health-insurance coverage altogether."*

Mental Health Should Not Be Treated on a Par with Physical Health

Richard E. Vatz

In the following viewpoint, Richard E. Vatz contends that giving mental illnesses and physical illnesses equal insurance coverage could lead to serious consequences. According to Vatz, insurance parity could lead to a destigmatization and subsequent increase in the use of psychoactive drugs. He also argues that full parity would be unaffordable. Vatz is a professor at Towson University in Towson, Maryland, and an associate psychology editor for *USA Today Magazine*.

As you read, consider the following questions:
1. In Vatz's opinion, what label makes drugs appear less dangerous?
2. How does Vatz respond to Tipper Gore's claim that she suffered "situational depression?"
3. What mental illness should be granted parity, according to the author?

Excerpted from "Overreach on Mental Health," by Richard E. Vatz, *The Washington Times*, June 23, 1999. Copyright ©1999 by News World Communications, Inc. Reprinted with the permission of *The Washington Times*.

[In June 1999] Tipper Gore completed the widely heralded first "White House Conference on Mental Health" whose agenda included most prominently what the administration's 1993 health-care proposal was unable to deliver: "parity" for "mental illness."

This goal also goes far beyond what mental health interests were able to accomplish in the Mental Health Parity Act of 1996. It means the claim of identity between mental and physical illness would finally be successful: any insurance company which insured mental illness would be required to insure such illness as they insure physical illness, with no limits on hospital stays or outpatient visits. Moreover, there could be no limits that would infringe on other health insurance coverage.

The American Psychiatric Association (APA) provides some idea of how many Americans should be seen as mentally ill or potentially mentally ill. The APA web site estimates that "between 15 and 25 percent of children evaluated in primary care settings have significant psychosocial disorders requiring some type of intervention." The APA web site also states unambiguously that "1 in 4 adults will suffer from a mental illness or substance abuse disorder in any year." The APA and the National Institute of Mental Health (NIMH) have indicated that more than 50 percent of all Americans will suffer from mental illness in their lifetime, and the Institute's Division of Epidemiology estimated that 52 million adults have a diagnosable mental illness, including substance abuse.

One of the consequences of "parity" coverage could be an exponential rise in the use of psychoactive drug usage. In fact, the very drugs that frighten parents of teen-agers are recommended by parity supporters with reassuring, palliative language: Mrs. Gore, in her recent public disclosure of being treated for depression, quoted unnamed "social worker friends" as saying "If Tipper Gore can take medication, I guess I can." When called "medication," drugs don't seem so dangerous.

It is ironic to note that the APA and Mrs. Gore's call for parity includes "substance use disorders," which is a medicalized way of saying "people who abuse drugs." The assumption that the use of drugs is not freely chosen behavior is a virtual guarantor of the perpetuation of such activity. But Mrs. Gore and the APA call the "drug abuse" label "stigmatizing" behavior, the most prominent bete noire of the mental health community. What they don't seem to acknowledge is that stigma has a salutary value as well. Tipper Gore's own confrontation with "mental illness," which she related [in May 1999], is illustrative.

Costly Coverage

Mandated mental health coverage would increase the cost of insurance. Estimates range from 2.5 percent to 8.7 percent in the first year. Although advocates believe that the lower range of these estimates would be inconsequential, when added to the annual increases in premiums of 8 percent or more that have become the norm, the burden would be far from negligible.

Mark Schiller, *New York Times*, June 15, 1999.

Mrs. Gore wrote of her "disease" of "situational depression" that she allegedly suffered pursuant to the life-threatening accident her 6-year-old suffered in 1989. There is no accepted mental illness recognized by the American Psychiatric Association called "situational depression," and depression following such a near-tragic experience, especially wherein one feels guilty regarding one's child's experience, is hardly unusual. Mrs. Gore refuses to discuss the drug or drugs she took as "therapy." Still, the stigma which attends psychoactive drug therapy, and which she vigorously attacks, can serve as a disincentive to those who would take such serious, mind-altering drugs for insufficient reasons.

Senators Pete Domenici and Paul Wellstone's "parity" bill, the Mental Health Equitable Treatment Act of 1999 (MHETA), requires that limitations on the coverage of benefits for "severe biologically based mental illnesses" may not be imposed unless comparable limitations are imposed on medical and surgical benefits. The National Alliance for the Mentally Ill (NAMI) claims that "the new bill provides full parity for people with serious brain disorders," which could well describe some cases of schizophrenia, but surely would not describe heretofore nonsevere mental illnesses, such as anorexia nervosa and attention deficit/hyperactivity disorder—both of which are now newly defined in the bill as "severe mental illnesses." The House bill even includes parity for substance abuse.

Through bait-and-switch labeling of the problems of the worried well plus the expansion of "severely mentally ill" category, the APA and Mrs. Gore's newly favored legislation creates an unjustified and unaffordable expansion of mental health benefits. The Employee Benefit Research Institute has determined that parity will lead eventually to increases in employer costs and possible elimination of other benefits in some cases, including health-insurance coverage altogether.

The NIMH estimates that 4.5 percent of Americans suffer from severe mental illness in a given year. If we take even that inflated figure seriously, we could come to an affordable national consensus on parity for mental disorders. If only correctly diagnosed (subject to serious utilization review), authentically severe mental illnesses, such as schizophrenia, manic depression and major depression, were granted parity there would not be the precipitous rise in health insurance costs and additional uninsured Americans that will result if mental health coverage is expanded to "full parity."

| "Many of the accommodations recommended for people with mental illness are simple and low-cost." |

The Mentally Ill Should Be Accommodated in the Workplace

Mary Conroy

In the following viewpoint, Mary Conroy asserts that laws requiring reasonable accommodations for mentally ill employees are necessary and do not create an unfair burden on employers. Conroy argues that mentally ill people are unfairly stigmatized and are entitled to perform their jobs in a supportive environment. Conroy is a freelance writer in Madison, Wisconsin.

As you read, consider the following questions:
1. According to Cathy Hazelbaker, as cited by the author, what five psychiatric illnesses have physical origins?
2. What were some of the fears of employers following the release of the Equal Employment Opportunity Commission guidelines, as stated by the author?
3. What misconception about mental illness has been influenced by movies, in Conroy's opinion?

Excerpted from "Workers with Mental Illness Deserve Support," by Mary Conroy, *Capital Times*, May 14, 1997. Reprinted with permission from the author.

An attorney had a form of schizophrenia. Like many schizophrenics, she could be very productive. In fact, she was very capable, but found it difficult to work in an open office with cubicles.

To work up to capacity, however, she needed her own room away from people. She wanted to be able to go to the room occasionally, shut the door and not work in a cubicle. It didn't have to be a fancy office with couches; it just had to be a quiet room.

Up until [spring 1997], her employer had no obligation to make that accommodation. Before then, the Americans with Disabilities Act of 1990 didn't clarify whether mentally ill employees were entitled to the same accommodations as, say, a person who uses a wheelchair.

But under the new guidelines the Equal Employment Opportunity Commission just ordered, employers may not discriminate against qualified workers if they have a mental illness. As a result, employers can't ask if a job applicant was ever mentally ill. In addition, employers must make reasonable accommodations for employees with mental illness, just as they do for physical illness.

Mental Illnesses Have Physical Origins

There's a basis for that parity, says Cathy Hazelbaker, administrator of the Alliance for the Mentally Ill of Dane County [in Wisconsin]. The five major psychiatric illnesses—bipolar illness, panic disorder, depression, schizophrenia and obsessive-compulsive disorder—have physical origins.

Studies of the brain have found either genetic bases for these illnesses, or have found that medication can treat abnormal levels of chemicals in the brain. Hazelbaker says we need to think of the brain as an organ like any other organ in the body. If the brain is sick, we make accommodations just as we would if someone in the office had diabetes.

Yet when the guidelines were issued, many employers went into a panic. They wondered whether they'd have to accommodate obsessive-compulsive employees who spent hours washing their hands. What would they do for warehouse employees loading boxes who come to work disheveled and anti-social? And what about workers who say they need time off for a mental disability—do they really, or are they just being slaggards?

Understanding the Guidelines

For one thing, Hazelbaker says, employees who spend hours washing their hands probably aren't being treated for their problem, because medication can put an end to such rituals. While employers can't force anyone to take medications, they can strongly encourage people to do so, while supporting them during their illness.

For another thing, the compliance guide issued by the EEOC says that employers have to consider whether workers' problems really affect the specific requirements of their jobs.

The Mentally Ill Can Be Productive

Those who suffer mental illness include the most productive members of society. Abraham Lincoln, recurrently depressed, is often mentioned, but mental illness is so common that examples are numberless. . . .

Some of my sicker patients are workers of extraordinary dedication who, for reasons related to their illness—compulsiveness and obsessional guilt—work scrupulously at tasks others avoid; smart employers do accommodate their needs.

Peter D. Kramer, *New York Times*, May 6, 1997.

Warehouse employees who have no contact with the public and come to work disheveled and anti-social can still pack boxes. A company dress code or a rule saying that employees should be courteous does not apply to a job packing boxes.

The day-off problem is a big fear of employers who wonder how difficult it is to diagnose a mental illness. But many mental illnesses are as easy to diagnose as low back pain, the No. 1 reason for claims filed under the Americans with Disabilities Act.

Besides, many of the accommodations recommended for people with mental illness are simple and low-cost. One employee may need a flexible work schedule to curb anxiety. Another may need to sit near a window to treat seasonal-affective disorder. And still another may need to see a psychiatrist for a 15-minute med check during the day.

Stigma Affects Treatment

Finally, we need to remember the huge stigma attached to mental illness. Some people are still so afraid of having their illness known that they pay for treatment themselves just so it won't go on their insurance records. Others simply don't get treatment.

It's unlikely that people performing poorly on the job will come out in droves saying, "I'm mentally ill, and that's why I'm acting this way on the job."

Personally, I think many people are simply afraid of people with mental illness. Movies and stories of violent criminals have given people the idea that mental illness is equated with violence. And no employer wants to hire someone who's violent.

Yet mentally ill people are all around us. They're our neighbors, our relatives, our co-workers. They hold down jobs, pay their taxes, help children with their homework. They take medication for depression and see their therapists.

They just want the same rights everyone else has—the right to do their best at work with employers who support them.

"How will workers react when they see chronically late, socially difficult, temperamental, or unlikable colleagues being given special privileges?"

Personality Disorders Should Not Be Accommodated in the Workplace

G.E. Zuriff

In the following viewpoint, G.E. Zuriff asserts that the Americans with Disabilities Act should not be used to accommodate employees with disruptive personalities. According to Zuriff, treating people with personality disorders on par with those who have physical disabilities would be costly to society and unfair to employers and coworkers. He concludes that employees who display character traits such as chronic lateness and poor tempers should be held morally responsible for their behavior. Zuriff is a professor of psychology at Wheaton College in Norton, Massachusetts, and a clinical psychologist in the medical department of the Massachusetts Institute of Technology in Cambridge, Massachusetts.

As you read, consider the following questions:
1. According to Zuriff, how many mood disorders are listed in the *Diagnostic and Statistical Manual of Mental Disorders*?
2. How many students with learning disabilities did the Individuals with Disabilities Education Act cover in 1992, according to the author?
3. In Zuriff's opinion, what do successful businesses understand?

Excerpted from "Medicalizing Character," by G.E. Zuriff, *The Public Interest*, no. 123, pp. 94–99, Spring 1996. Copyright ©1996 by National Affairs, Inc. Reprinted with the permission of the author and *The Public Interest*.

Hailed as "the most far-reaching legislation ever enacted against discrimination of people with disabilities," the Americans with Disabilities Act (ADA) extends the civil-rights protections of individuals with disabilities to employment, public accommodations, transportation, government services, and telecommunications. Not only is discrimination outlawed but businesses and public facilities must make "reasonable" changes to accommodate disabilities, unless "undue hardship" would result.

When most Americans think of the ADA, they imagine people in wheelchairs or with visual impairments working productively, attending college for the first time, or using accessible buses, all because the law now requires that their special needs be met. However, within disability laws are provisions going beyond these inspirational images and threatening to undermine our culture's already fragile sense of personal responsibility.

Not surprisingly, the ADA's definition of a disability includes a variety of physical disorders, but it is less well known that the definition also includes "mental impairment that substantially limits one or more major life activities." In fact, during the first 15 months of the ADA, nearly 10 percent of all violation complaints concerned mental disabilities, second only to back problems. Unfortunately, however, "mental impairment" is not well defined within either the ADA or psychiatry.

Defining Disorders

Federal regulations attempt to clarify by stating that "mental impairment means any mental or psychological disorder such as mental retardation, organic brain syndrome, emotional or mental illness." Yet no regulation specifies what constitutes an emotional or mental illness. Nevertheless, when we look at the legislative history of the ADA, the opinions of experts in the field, and ADA court cases, we find a consensus that the *Diagnostic and Statistical Manual of Mental Disorders (DSM)*, first published by the American Psychiatric Association in 1952 and now in its fourth edition, is the definitive guide. This tome provides the official names, descriptions, and diagnostic criteria for hundreds of psychological disorders.

Perusing the *DSM* is an eye opener. Of course, we find mental retardation (five varieties) and schizophrenia (also in five varieties), but we also encounter oppositional defiant disorder, anxiety disorders (11 types), and mood disorders (17 types). Most disturbing in their practical and moral implications are the 11 categories of "personality disorders." For example, the "narcissistic personality disorder" consists of "a pervasive pattern of grandiosity (in fantasy or behavior), need for admiration, and lack of empathy . . . present in a variety of contexts, as indicated by five (or more) of the following." What follows is a list of nine personality traits, including that the person has a grandiose sense of self-importance, believes that he is "special," requires excessive admiration, takes advantage of others, lacks empathy, is envious of others, and shows arrogant attitudes. For the "obsessive-compulsive personality disorder," we find "a pervasive pattern of preoccupation with orderliness, perfectionism, and mental and interpersonal control, at the expense of flexibility, openness, and efficiency." The person disabled by an "avoidant personality disorder" shows "a pervasive pattern of social inhibition, feelings of inadequacy, and hypersensitivity to negative evaluation."

What were in earlier times considered to be faults of mind and flaws of character are today regarded as "psychological disorders," which are, moreover, covered by the ADA. If an employee can show, for example, that an inability to relate well to co-workers is a direct result of a narcissistic personality disorder, then the employer is not only forbidden to dismiss the worker but must also make reasonable accommodations for this "disability."

Frightening Implications

The social implications of treating personality disorders on a par with physical disabilities are momentous. First, we do not know how many people meet the *DSM* diagnostic criteria and can, therefore, demand legal accommodation. The *DSM* estimates the prevalence of each of its personality-disorder categories at about 2 percent of the population, creating the potential for 10 million to 20 million Americans requiring accommodations in work, school, and public facilities because of their personalities.

If the experience with the Individuals with Disabilities Education Act (IDEA) is any indication, we are in for a frightening future. Once a diagnosis of the psychological disorder "learning disability" became an admission ticket to a variety of entitlements and civil rights under IDEA, the number of diagnoses exploded. During the first year of IDEA (1976), students with learning disabilities comprised less than 24 percent of all disabled children covered; by 1992, they constituted 52.4 percent. These 2,369,385 learning disabled students received over $1 billion in benefits. In recent years, the annual increases in the number of disabled students under IDEA is almost totally attributable to the growth in the number of learning disabled children. It will be interesting to see if the number of personality-disorder diagnoses similarly skyrockets as the ADA works its way into public consciousness.

Gary Brookins for the *Richmond Times-Dispatch*. Reprinted with permission.

A more serious question concerns the effects on the moral fabric of our society as character faults come to be viewed as no different from physical disabilities. What happens to a society that accommodates people who are excessively narcissistic, antisocial, histrionic, dependent, or compulsive rather than insisting that they accommodate themselves to society? How will workers react when they see chronically late, socially difficult, temperamental, or unlikable colleagues being given special privileges? What will workers think of sensitivity-training sessions that encourage them to tolerate, and even empathize with, a co-worker who is rude or lacks self-control? . . .

Clarify the Definitions of Disability

What is to be done? First, new regulations must clarify and further limit the definition of mental disability. Congress's handling of sexual disorders, drug addiction, and alcoholism can serve as a model. Although all three appear in the *DSM*, the ADA explicitly excludes sexual disorders from coverage, includes drug addiction only under very circumscribed conditions, and limits coverage of alcoholism. Similar qualifications are in order for other mental disorders. While it may make some sense to protect and accommodate people with schizophrenia who lack control over their illness, the same is not true for people with personality disorders. Their actions, attitudes, and qualities of character are commonly disapproved of in our society, and they should be held morally responsible for them. They should be encouraged to accommodate to society rather than the reverse. At the same time, we can recognize their suffering and perhaps help provide them with the appropriate psychotherapy.

While limiting the application of the ADA, we should not lose sight of some of its good intentions. Successful businesses have come to understand that good management means recognizing psychological differences among employees and creating working environments that maximize each individual's potential. Often this means tailoring jobs to fit an employee's weaknesses, as well as strengths, even if this entails some expense in providing the necessary supports. This is the sort of enlightened self-interest that employers have to some extent practiced even without the ADA. Thus there is reason to hope that a reformed and narrowed ADA, coupled with competitive market forces, will bring about a more humane, productive workplace.

Periodical Bibliography

The following articles have been selected to supplement the diverse views presented in this chapter. Addresses are provided for periodicals not indexed in the *Readers' Guide to Periodical Literature*, the *Alternative Press Index*, the *Social Sciences Index*, or the *Index to Legal Periodicals and Books*.

J. Wesley Boyd
"Managed Care Folly—Time to End the Silence?" *The Pharos*, Fall 1998. Available from Alpha Omega Alpha Honor Medical Society, 525 Middlefield Road, Suite 130, Menlo Park, CA 94025.

John Cloud
"Mental Health Reform: What It Would Really Take," *Time*, June 7, 1999.

Theodore Dalrymple
"Ill Deeds Aren't a Sign of Ill Health," *Wall Street Journal*, April 23, 1998.

William Goldman, Joyce McCulloch, and Roland Sturm
"Costs and Use of Mental Health Services Before and After Managed Care," *Health Affairs*, March/April 1998. Available from Project HOPE, 7500 Old Georgetown Road, Suite 600, Bethesda, MD 20814-6133.

Daniel J. Judiscak
"Why Are the Mentally Ill in Jail?" *American Jails*, November/December 1995. Available from the American Jail Association, 2053 Day Road, Suite 100, Hagerstown, MD 21740-9795.

Peter D. Kramer
"The Mentally Ill Deserve Job Protection," *New York Times*, May 6, 1997.

Penelope Lemov
"Legislating to Prozac," *Governing*, December 1996.

Geanne Rosenberg
"When the Mind Is the Matter: Mental Disability Cases Pose Painful Workplace Issues," *New York Times*, November 7, 1998.

Carl Rowan
"Can the White House De-Stigmatize Mental Illness?" *Liberal Opinion Week*, June 21, 1999. Available from PO Box 880, Vinton, IA 52349-0880.

Nina Schuyler
"Out of the Shadows," *In These Times*, February 8, 1998.

E. Fuller Torrey and Mary T. Zdanowicz
"We've Tried Mandatory Treatment—and It Works," *City Journal*, Summer 1999. Available from the Manhattan Institute, 52 Vanderbilt Avenue, New York, NY 10017.

Richard E. Vatz and Lee S. Weinberg
"Should Mental Illness Fall Under the Americans with Disabilities Act?" *USA Today*, January 1999.

Richard E. Vatz
and Lee S. Weinberg

"The Insanity Defense: Unconscionable Impact
on Victims of Violence," *USA Today*, May 1998.

Michael Winerip

"Bedlam on the Streets," *New York Times
Magazine*, May 23, 1999.

Gordon Witkin

"What Does It Take to Be Crazy?" *U.S. News &
World Report*, January 12, 1998.

CHAPTER 3

What Mental Health Issues Do Children Face?

Chapter Preface

Until the middle of the twentieth century, it was generally believed that children were not affected by mental disorders. Today, however, most medical professionals agree that nearly every mental disorder present in adults can affect children as well. The Institute of Medicine estimates that 12 percent of children in the United States—about 7.5 million boys and girls under the age of eighteen—have some type of brain disorder.

Before it was accepted that children could suffer from mental illnesses, many people believed that a child's emotional and behavioral problems were the result of outside factors, such as bad parenting. Parents were advised that such problems would disappear if they exerted more discipline, or if mothers stayed at home with their young children, or if fathers were more attentive. Some people even believed that the children's problems were the result of being weaned too early. Over and over, parents were told that they were the reason behind their children's problems.

Today, most doctors, therapists, and parents believe that many children's emotional and behavioral problems are actually symptoms of mental disorders that are the result of chemical imbalances in the brain. Harold S. Koplewicz, director of the division of child and adolescent psychiatry at New York University Medical Center, emphasizes that parents are not to blame for their child's psychiatric disorder.

> Children with brain disorders . . . have these disorders largely because of the way their brains work. The fact that the symptoms of these disorders are behavioral doesn't change the fact that there is a neurobiological basis to them. Parents are no more to "blame" for a child's psychiatric disorder than they are to "blame" for his epilepsy or his red hair.

Two of the most commonly diagnosed mental disorders in children are attention deficit hyperactivity disorder and depression. The authors in the following chapter examine the prevalence of ADHD and debate whether drug treatments for ADHD and depression are safe and effective for children.

> *"Parents should also be mindful that the adverse effects of* not *taking a drug are often far more unpleasant than the possible side effects of taking it."*

Antidepressants Are Helpful for Depressed Children

Harold S. Koplewicz

Fear of side effects and the stigma of brain disorders keep many parents from medicating their children for their mental disorders. Harold S. Koplewicz argues in the following viewpoint, however, that mental disorders are serious afflictions that prevent children from leading normal lives. Medicating children for brain disorders can make their lives easier and healthier, he asserts. In fact, Koplewicz contends, the effects of not medicating a child for a brain disorder are frequently worse than any side effects from the drugs used to treat it. Koplewicz is the author of *It's Nobody's Fault: New Hope and Help for Difficult Children and Their Parents*, from which this viewpoint is taken.

As you read, consider the following questions:
1. What is Koplewicz's response to those who claim that medication for brain disorders is a crutch?
2. What are some long-term effects of untreated brain disorders, according to Koplewicz?
3. What is the parents' responsibility when a child is diagnosed with a brain disorder, in the author's view?

According to his mother, 10-year-old Adam had always been a "difficult child." When Adam and his parents came to my office for the first time, I learned that the little boy had been seeing a psychologist three times a week for five years. That's roughly *750 sessions*. Adam was still having serious trouble with his behavior. He wasn't doing well in school, and he didn't have any friends to speak of. I asked the parents what had taken them so long to bring their child to a psychiatrist.

"Well, Adam's psychologist has been telling us for several years that he probably needs medication for his attention deficit hyperactivity disorder, but we were afraid to do it," the mother replied. "We thought that it would change his personality," added the father. "And besides, we don't like the idea of medicating a child."

I've met a lot of parents who don't like the idea of medicating a child for a brain disorder—or anything else, for that matter—but that was the first time I had ever encountered parents who preferred 750 sessions of psychotherapy that didn't work to a daily dose of medication that does work. After two weeks of a moderate dose of Ritalin Adam was a lot better. His parents, his teacher, and his friends noticed the change right away.

Fooling Mother Nature

Adam's parents are not alone, of course. Many fathers and mothers are adamantly opposed to the idea of psychopharmacology for their children. "My kid on drugs? *Never!*" is something I've heard more than a few times. Parents who wouldn't think twice about giving their children insulin to treat diabetes or an inhaler to ease the symptoms of asthma balk at the prospect of giving their child medication for a mental disorder, for any number of reasons. They worry that the child will become addicted to the medication or will be encouraged to abuse other drugs. They fear that the child will be stigmatized by taking medication. They're concerned about the negative side effects. Some parents regard giving a child medication as taking the easy way out. They think that a more "natural" approach—for example, withholding sugar and caffeine, or using discipline, or trying to get to the root cause of every problem—is the more desirable, even the morally superior, course of treatment.

"Isn't it a crutch?" some concerned parents ask, and I have to say yes, I suppose medication is a kind of crutch. But if a child's leg is broken, what's wrong with a crutch? If a youngster has a broken limb, he can't be expected to get around without some help. If a child has an infection, doesn't he take antibiotics? If a child's brain isn't functioning the way it's supposed to, shouldn't he be given whatever assistance is available to make it easier for him to lead a normal life, free of distress and dysfunction? Parents have to understand that brain disorders must be taken as seriously as asthma, diabetes, or any other organic problem. A child with a brain disorder is suffering, and there is nothing wrong with using medication to relieve a child's suffering.

Many parents who come to see me don't need to be persuaded about the virtues of medication. This is especially true of parents who have been helped by some of these medications themselves. When I recently prescribed a low dosage of Zoloft, an antidepressant, for a little girl with selective mutism, her parents didn't hesitate for a moment to follow my advice. "You know, a year ago I started taking Zoloft for depression, and it completely changed my life," the little girl's mother said. "There was a time I would never have dreamed of giving my child psychiatric medicine, but I don't feel that way anymore."

The father of a little boy with severe obsessive compulsive disorder put his feelings about medication even more succinctly: "Our son's life began the day he started taking his medicine."

The Stigma of Medicine

It's all very well for my colleagues and me to equate brain disorders with diabetes and to say that giving a child Ritalin shouldn't be any different from making sure he takes his insulin. We know that there *is* a difference. A pediatrician looks in a child's ears, detects an infection, and prescribes ampicillin. Parents give the child his medicine without missing a beat. Do they ask the pediatrician about its long-term side effects or question him closely about what caused the infection? Probably not, or at least not at any length. They might even tell their friends about it. There's no stigma attached to having an ear infection. Most parents won't keep a child's diabetes a secret. There is, unfortunately, a stigma attached to having a brain disorder, and as a result many parents are secretive about their children's problems and the fact that they're taking medication.

When I hear stories of how some people react, I can't really blame parents for keeping the news to themselves. One worried mother called me because the principal at her child's school said her son shouldn't be taking the Ritalin I had prescribed (and to which he was responding wonderfully well). The Ritalin is a crutch, the principal said; what the child really needed was a lighter school schedule and a different teacher. I was shocked by the principal's ignorance, not to mention his colossal nerve. If I had prescribed two puffs of an inhaler to keep a child with asthma from wheezing during gym class, I doubt that the principal would have suggested that the child forget the medicine and be excused from gym instead.

Another mother showed up at my office in tears. Her daughter's teacher had told her that medicine—in this case an antidepressant for separation anxiety disorder—is the worst possible thing for a growing child. "I can't believe you're giving her drugs," the teacher said to the mother. (This was the same teacher who, only a few months earlier, had told the mother that her six-year-old daughter Ellen had some real problems, that all she did all day in class was stare down at her desk, cry, and ask to go home to her mommy.) Ellen's mother sputtered a response to the teacher: "But you told me there was a problem. I'm trying to fix it." The teacher's response: "I told you to do something, but I didn't mean this." The fact that with the medication Ellen was able to attend class all day without chronic worries and fears didn't affect the teacher's attitude. . . .

The Side Effects

"What will this medicine do to my kid?" is almost always the first question that passes any parent's lips, and it's a good one. If a child with a fever takes too much Tylenol, it may cause inflammation of the kidneys. The ampicillin that cures a child's ear infection often causes diarrhea. All medicines, including those prescribed for children's brain disorders, have side effects, and parents should know in advance what to expect.

However, parents should also be mindful that the adverse effects of *not* taking a drug are often far more unpleasant than the possible side effects of taking it. The long-term effects of an *untreated* brain disorder—distress, low self-esteem, dropping out of school, unsatisfying interpersonal relationships, and many others—can be truly devastating.

Prozac Works

Andrew Crittendon was only 7 when an inexplicable bleakness descended on him. "I lost interest in everything," he recalls. "I just sat in my room and thought about how horrible life was." Andrew's mother, Beverly, started to worry when a trip to Six Flags Great Adventure didn't lift his spirits, and her concern turned to terror when the child started talking about suicide. Dr. Graham Emslie, the Dallas-based psychiatrist who diagnosed Andrew's depression, offered to enroll him in a study of Prozac. "I didn't care what they did," Andrew says, "as long as there was a chance it would make me feel better." It did—and he stayed on the drug for four years. At 11, he discovered he no longer needed it. Andrew is now a six-foot-tall ninth grader with his sights set on a career in filmmaking. "I'm really one of the happiest people I know," he says.

Mary Crowley, *Newsweek*, October 20, 1997.

Little Billy, a seven-year-old child with a brain disorder—attention deficit hyperactivity disorder—comes to me in severe distress and obvious dysfunction. He's inattentive, hyperactive, agitated. He can't focus on anything in school, and he drives everyone crazy with his obnoxious behavior. His teacher doesn't like him; the other kids don't want to play with him; even his parents find his behavior intolerable. He's the only one in the class who doesn't get invited to the birthday parties. He's not learning anything, and he's not having any fun. With the correct dose of a stimulant he can focus in school and follow the lessons. He can play with his friends and go places with his parents.

To be sure, the stimulant may cause a decrease in little Billy's appetite, alter his sleep patterns slightly, or cause an occasional headache. But without the stimulant this child is heading for trouble that's a lot more serious than a headache. To me the choice seems clear: the child needs the medication.

The Bottom Line

A colleague of mine says that the most important task that children have is to choose the right parents. Carefully chosen parents not only accept their children's assets and deficits; they also do whatever is necessary to make sure that their kids have plenty of opportunities to use their assets and are given whatever help they need to compensate for those deficits. That's what parenting is all about.

A child's brain disorder is not a parent's fault, but finding the right treatment for the disorder is a parent's responsibility. If a son is diagnosed with diabetes, it is a parent's job to give the child his medication, work out a proper diet, and give him the moral support he needs to keep himself well. If a daughter has an allergy, a parent should make sure she takes her shots, keep the house allergen-free, and offer moral support. The same rules apply to a brain disorder. A parent's job is to find the right treatment, work with the doctor and the child to implement it, build the child's self-confidence, and make the child's life easier along the way. Often the right treatment will include medication.

There are hundreds of thousands of success stories associated with pediatric psychopharmacology. "We got our life back" and "We finally could think about having another child" and "It was a miracle" are the kinds of comments heard every day from parents whose children's lives have been turned around by medication. Like Adam's parents, who took their child to a therapist 750 times before deciding to give medicine a try, they probably don't *like* the idea of giving a child medicine, but they like it a lot more than the alternative.

"No doubt there are children and teenagers who could genuinely benefit from antidepressants. But it's easy to see how millions might wind up taking antidepressants as a false cure for childhood and adolescence."

Antidepressants for Children Are Overprescribed

Arianna Huffington

Prozac is a drug commonly prescribed to treat depression. In the following viewpoint, Arianna Huffington asserts that more and more children are being prescribed antidepressants such as Prozac without undergoing thorough psychiatric evaluations first. These examinations are necessary, she maintains, because many normal children exhibit behaviors that are similar to the symptoms used to describe depression. Although antidepressants do benefit some children and teenagers, Huffington believes that these drugs are being used to "cure" the typical problems of adolescence. Huffington is a nationally syndicated columnist.

As you read, consider the following questions:

1. How many children are prescribed antidepressants, as cited by the author?
2. According to Huffington, how is Eli Lilly trying to make Prozac more palatable to children?
3. How will society soon come to view mood disorders, according to Barbara Ingersoll as cited by the author?

Excerpted from "Peppermint Prozac," by Arianna Huffington, *U.S. News & World Report*, August 18–25, 1997. Copyright ©1997 by U.S. News & World Report.

Is your daughter depressed about acne? Soon, you may be able to take her to a dermatologist for peppermint-flavored Prozac. Is your son blue over an ingrown toenail? Take him to a podiatrist for some antidepressants. Is he angry about having to wear braces? His orthodontist may soon be handing out pills along with a dinosaur toothbrush.

Already, at least 580,000 children are being prescribed antidepressants—and those numbers are likely to increase dramatically. For now, doctors can prescribe Prozac to kids but Eli Lilly, which manufactures the drug, can't market it as a children's remedy. According to the *Medical Sciences Bulletin*, however, "the FDA is currently evaluating Prozac for use as an antidepressant in children." If the FDA gives its blessing, Eli Lilly will be free to peddle "children's" Prozac—especially now that the FDA is about to clear the way for TV advertising of prescription drugs. The company already has on the market a peppermint-flavored version of Prozac. And where Prozac leads, other antidepressants, such as Zoloft and Paxil, are sure to follow.

Doctors may prescribe antidepressants to children without any psychiatric evaluation. Yet the symptoms used to identify depression in a recent Prozac ad range from feeling "unusually sad or irritable" to finding it "hard to concentrate." I have two healthy little girls, ages 6 and 8, both of whom have experienced these symptoms. Indeed, I don't know any normal children who haven't.

No doubt there are children and teenagers who could genuinely benefit from antidepressants. But it's easy to see how millions might wind up taking antidepressants as a false cure for childhood and adolescence. One father in Southern California wrote to me recently to say that one of his son's friends is on antidepressants "because her parents are 'too strict' and she is depressed at not being able to do what other kids do."

A Passing Cloud

Signs of depression may be nothing more than a passing cloud—or an indication of unresolved grief and loss. A doctor spending a few minutes with a child cannot possibly know the difference. "It's part of the human condition to feel crummy if something bad is happening in one's life," says Harold Koplewicz, vice chairman of psychiatry at the New York University Medical Center. "But that is very different from having a clinical disorder."

Indeed, substituting the quick fix of a drug for the often frustrating reality of parenting can be a subtle form of child abuse. It is our job as parents to help our kids navigate life's emotional roller coaster. Their mental health depends not only on their life experiences—good and bad—but on how they learn to cope with them.

Children behave notoriously in line with the expectations of the adults around them. If we think they can't cope without a pill, they will grow up believing that. If we teach our children that pills will make them feel better, how can we then tell them not to try a joint or a few drinks to lift their spirits?

Hot Pills

Kids' prescriptions for Prozac-type drugs rose by 80 percent in 2 years.

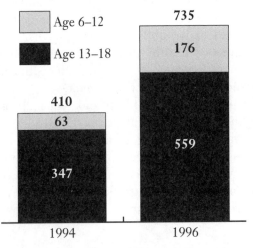

prescriptions, in thousands

Age 6–12

Age 13–18

735
176

410
63
347

559

1994   1996

Mary Crowley, *Newsweek*, October 20, 1997.

It may not be long before stressed parents and teachers, bombarded with ads promising immediate relief for their kids—and themselves—will turn to Prozac with alarming frequency. Forty percent of American children live without a father in the house. How tempting antidepressants will seem to those overwhelmed mothers.

One psychologist, Barbara Ingersoll, recently proclaimed that before long "mood disorders will be treated not as exotic, uncommon conditions in children but more like (cavities) or poor vision . . . There won't be a stigma for kids on Prozac—the stigma will be on not taking Prozac." In the past, the upper classes typically dealt with the stresses of childhood by sending their kids to boarding school. Now, instead of being sent to Hotchkiss, children can be transported to Camp Prozac.

There are so many forces pushing us to accelerate the use of antidepressants for children. But we need to slow down. "Children are so vulnerable," says Michael Faenza, president and CEO of the National Mental Health Association. "We don't have a good body of research yet about how antidepressants will affect them long term." Even in Aldous Huxley's *Brave New World*, Soma—the drug that kept everyone manageably numb—wasn't put in the kids' bottles.

A Modest Solution

Here is a modest solution. Until much more is known about the effects of antidepressants on children's brains, why can't doctors simply refuse to prescribe the drugs without a full psychiatric evaluation? Since Eli Lilly claims to be concerned primarily with the mental health of its customers—as opposed to opening an enormous new market for Prozac—company executives would no doubt agree to such a restriction. And if they find that pill too hard to swallow, maybe the FDA could give it to them in a nice peppermint-flavored version.

> "[Attention Deficit Hyperactivity Disorder]
> is part of our genetic legacy, a variation in
> brain functioning which affects millions of
> people in this country and around the
> world."

Childhood Attention Deficit Disorder Is a Serious Problem

Peter Jaksa

Attention deficit disorder (ADD) is characterized by short attention spans, impulsiveness, and in the case of ADHD, hyperactivity. In the following viewpoint, Peter Jaksa asserts that ADD and ADHD are genetic brain conditions that have been misunderstood for decades. ADD/ADHD present real problems for people, and the disorders are not a "myth," as claimed by some so-called experts, Jaksa contends. When properly diagnosed and treated, people with these disorders can lead relatively normal lives. Jaksa is a psychologist and president of the National Attention Deficit Disorder Association.

As you read, consider the following questions:
1. What was the first name given to Attention Deficit Disorder, according to Jaksa?
2. How are critics of ADD/ADHD regarded by their professional communities, according to the author?
3. What types of treatment does Jaksa recommend for people with ADHD?

People with Attention Deficit Disorder have been taken on a wild ride over the past 40 years. As recently as 1964, Attention Deficit Hyperactivity Disorder (ADHD) was so poorly understood that it was labeled MBD, for "Minimal Brain Damage." We know now that this genetic, inherited condition is not due to brain damage at all but rather to a variation in how the brain functions in approximately five percent of the population. In 1968 the name was changed to "Hyperkinetic Reaction of Childhood," because the focus was on hyperactive children who had a lot of trouble sitting still in the classroom and getting their work done. In 1980 the name was changed again to "Attention Deficit Disorder" because it became recognized that severe attention problems and poor impulse control were major defining characteristics as well. It also became clear through research studies, years of clinical experience, and the reports of many adults, that ADHD did not go away after childhood but continued to profoundly effect many people in their adult lives.

A Changing Understanding

The latest term in the evolution of the medical terminology is ADHD, or "Attention Deficit Hyperactivity Disorder." The name changes over the years reflect our growing understanding of this condition and advances in science, medicine, education, and disability legislation. When properly diagnosed, ADHD is a highly treatable condition that responds well to certain medications and to behavioral management in the classroom, workplace, and home. If not treated adequately, ADHD can cause havoc in a person's life. Untreated ADHD often results in chronic education, work, and career problems, difficult relationships, increased risk of substance abuse, and loss of faith in oneself despite the best of intentions and very hard effort. If properly diagnosed and treated, people with ADHD lead lives as happy and productive as anyone else. There are many positive qualities associated with ADHD, as well as potentially serious difficulties that need to be understood and worked with.

All of the above progress and good news is being threatened to be undone by an unexpected development: ADHD has become a "diagnosis du jour" of sorts, as well as a hot media topic. Local and national newspapers, magazines, and TV programs have featured stories on ADHD and on Ritalin, the most publicized (but not the ONLY) medication used in the treatment of ADHD. Ritalin, a stimulant medication that has been around for decades, has been featured on the covers of *Time* magazine, parent magazines, the *Chicago Tribune Magazine*, and discussed on national TV and radio programs. While some benefits of treatment are noted, there is a troubling darker tone to many of these media stories that plays up to people's fears and apprehensions about ADHD and taking medications. In particular, they play up to the apprehension and guilt many parents experience when it comes to giving their children medication.

Contriving a Controversy

More recently the media focus has been on a number of books written by self-proclaimed experts that cover the "controversy" about ADHD and Ritalin. Some of these books argue for still another definition: that ADHD is a "myth," a social invention, a figment of imagination pushed by the health professions, teachers and educators, and advocacy organizations such as CHADD (Children And Adults With Attention Deficit Disorders). The national organizations, so goes a repeated conspiracy theory, are supported and influenced by the pharmaceutical companies. How then can you trust anything these organizations tell you? In particular, the parent-based organization CHADD has been repeatedly smeared by innuendo that financial contributions from drug companies have tainted the organization's objectivity and influenced policy. These claims are silly and unfair, but still toxic in their effect in breeding mistrust and suspicion. The advocacy organizations such as ADDA and CHADD sponsor conferences where researchers and professionals can present their findings, but nobody tells the presenters what to present. They review research, but nobody tells academic or medical researchers what to study or how to conduct the research.

The erstwhile "experts" who write highly sensationalistic books about the "myth" of ADHD and exaggerate the dangers of medication enjoy little respect within their professional communities. This is probably for good reason, because their claims don't have any scientific base or substantive evidence to back them up. The kindest thing I can say about these books, as a psychologist who has worked with children and adults with ADHD for over a decade, and as an adult who himself is diagnosed with ADHD, is that the claims made in these books are highly dubious and not taken seriously by those who are knowledgeable about ADHD. People who live with ADHD and parents of children with ADHD know that these books are mostly nonsense and hype. We cannot, and will not, turn back decades of scientific research on the biological basis of ADHD, medical research, educational progress, and federal disability legislation, because some people selling books are claiming that ADHD is a "myth."

Amazingly, some members of the media seem drawn to these books and authors like moths to flames. The media, as Dr. Thomas Phelan and others have pointed out, loves controversy or whatever passes for controversy. The "myth" of ADHD has itself become a topic du jour. An author who questions the legitimacy of ADHD, and the safety or effectiveness of medication, provides plenty of controversy that creates headlines and interesting stories. Every print, TV, radio journalist, or amateur novelist knows that conflict creates interest. When a scientist or medical expert writes a book on ADHD and summarizes the accumulated scientific and medical knowledge, that paints one picture of what ADHD is about. If, however, you find a few opposing voices (easily done) then you have a controversy brewing. Controversy generates interest, newspapers and magazines get sold, TV shows get promoted, and the issue becomes part of a media circus. While the entertainment value of such stories cannot be doubted, accuracy and responsible reporting take a hit.

Ritalin

A cover story in *Time* magazine proclaims this "The Age Of Ritalin." Actually a more accurate assessment might be, "the age of media overkill and hype about Ritalin." The scientific and medical evidence is thrown in with the usual stereotypes, hype, and social angst about what taking Ritalin entails for the social fabric. A cover story on ADHD in the *Chicago Tribune Magazine* shows a bottle of Ritalin along with the headline "Is A Pill The Answer For A Society That Can't Concentrate?" Of course the answer is "no," but the question itself is bogus and meaningless. ADHD is not a "social condition" or cultural phenomenon, societies don't suffer from it, and societies cannot be treated for it. ADHD is a biological, genetic condition that is experienced by individuals. Those individuals can indeed be treated by their physicians, psychologists, counselors, and other health care providers.

Report Concludes ADHD Is Not Over-diagnosed

There is "little evidence of widespread overdiagnosis or misdiagnosis of ADHD [attention deficit hyperactivity disorder] or of overprescription of methylphenidate by physicians," declares a report published in the April 8, 1998, *Journal of the American Medical Association*. Conducted by the AMA's Council on Scientific Affairs, the report is based on a review of all English-language studies examining children from elementary through high school age. Its findings repudiate allegations and public concern that "the diagnosis [of ADHD] is merely applied to control children who exhibit unwanted behaviors."

The number of children and adults who have been diagnosed with ADHD and treated with methylphenidate [a drug more commonly known as Ritalin] has risen significantly over the past decade. This increase has spurred concern that the diagnosis is made too frequently and without merit and that methylphenidate, which accounts for more than 90 percent of stimulant used to treat ADHD in the U.S., is being prescribed too often to treat these children. According to the report, however, the increase in the diagnosis and treatment of ADHD can be attributed mainly to an "increase in the recognition of the disorder and a refinement of the diagnostic criteria," which has resulted in more girls being diagnosed and an expanding appreciation of the persistence of ADHD into adulthood.

Lisa Horan, *Attention!* 1998, vol. 5, no. 1.

Treating ADHD, or Ritalin and other medications used to treat ADHD, as a cultural phenomenon or a "myth" and not as a biological condition creates doubt, confusion, and apprehension for many people with ADHD. It also creates doubts and confusion for those who live with them, work with them, or teach them. I am alarmed every time I encounter a teacher, for example, who has decided that "I don't believe in ADHD." What, pray tell, has your school system been teaching you then? Even worse, what is going to happen to a child with ADHD who ends up in your classroom? If I'm the parent, that child is out of the teacher's classroom as soon as I'm aware of the teacher's bias and ignorance. Next would come a talk with the principal and the school board.

Individuals with ADHD need accurate information and help, not smoke screens, pseudo-theories, and scare tactics. Treatment involves increasing awareness and learning more coping skills (always), and taking medication (often but not always) which improves attention and helps control other symptoms. We know what effective, safe treatment is on the basis of hundreds of research studies and decades of clinical experience. We must not scare people away from what is safe and effective and push them towards things that hold no proven benefits for ADHD, such as vitamin, herbal, or diet strategies, or confuse people so much that they seek no treatment at all. People with ADHD need to be understood and accepted, not to be labeled as fakers or slackers by those who lack understanding.

Demoralized and Frustrated Children

As a psychologist, I have worked with hundreds of children with ADHD who are demoralized and frustrated because, without treatment, they could not pay attention well enough to get their schoolwork done, or could not control their disruptive and impulsive behavior well enough to avoid getting into trouble repeatedly. When you ask them why they think these problems happen, many will tell you, with sadness and shame, that they are "lazy," or "stupid," or simply "bad." This is the only explanation they have, because it's what they often hear from others around them who may not know any better.

It can be a tremendous source of understanding and relief to learn that the problem behaviors have a biological basis and are not due to character defects or lack of effort. Treatment provides hope, and better behavioral control, which translates to more responsible and productive behavior. If behavioral methods are not enough by themselves, then medication should be carefully considered by the person's physician and, in the case of a child, by the parents. It is never appropriate for a teacher, or parents acting on their own, to make decisions about using or not using medication. The use of medication is a medical issue, although at times it has been portrayed as a "social issue" or media controversy. We hear nothing about the "controversy" of giving insulin to people with diabetes, or anti-seizure medications to people with a seizure disorder. Thankfully, diabetes and seizure disorders are recognized as biological conditions and not treated as controversial topics or "myths." We would all be better off to hold ADHD in the same light.

A Genetic Legacy

Media professionals have a responsibility to avoid spreading myths and fears about ADHD, and to provide accurate and realistic coverage. ADHD is not a disease or illness, it is not brain damage, and it certainly is not a "myth." It is part of our human genetic legacy, a variation in brain functioning which affects millions of people in this country and around the world. It is not a simple phenomenon, hence some of the confusion and controversies around it. We need more and better efforts to increase public awareness about ADHD, and to treat ADHD safely and effectively for those who live with it. It is highly irresponsible and damaging to these efforts to promote nonsense theories that have no scientific basis and no substantive evidence for them.

Understanding ADHD requires doing plenty of homework, reviewing the available knowledge, and putting it in perspective. The accumulated body of knowledge about ADHD took a great deal of time and effort to come by, and cannot be dismissed because someone considers it a "myth." Please avoid too easy or quick generalizations, because you will almost surely be wrong. Finally, be reminded that when you write about ADHD you are writing about people. ADHD is part of many people's lives, part of their biology, and part of their identity. Treat it with respect—and care.

> *"I wonder whether this 'disorder' really exists in the child at all, or whether, more properly, it exists in the relationships that are present between the child and his or her environment."*

The Extent of Childhood Attention Deficit Disorder Is Exaggerated

Thomas Armstrong

In the following viewpoint, Thomas Armstrong questions the existence and prevalence of attention deficit disorder (ADD) which is characterized by overactivity, impulsiveness, and inattentiveness. According to Armstrong, a child's symptoms of ADD may appear in one setting only to disappear when the child is involved in novel, interesting, or stimulating situations. In addition, the method used to determine whether a child has ADD is extremely subjective, he contends, and could be influenced by the observers' preconceived notions about the child. Thomas concludes that the acceptance of ADD by the educational community is especially troublesome due to the stigma attached to such a diagnosis. Armstrong is the author of *The Myth of the ADD Child*.

As you read, consider the following questions:

1. According to the concerned mother quoted by the author, how will a change in the definition of ADD affect the prevalence of the disorder?
2. According to Armstrong, why did the NEA and NASP oppose the classification of ADD as a legal handicap?

Excerpted from "ADD: Does It Really Exist?" by Thomas Armstrong, *Phi Delta Kappan*, February 1996. Reprinted with permission from the author.

S everal years ago I worked for an organization that assisted teachers in using the arts in their classrooms. We were located in a large warehouse in Cambridge, Massachusetts, and several children from the surrounding lower-working-class neighborhood volunteered to help with routine jobs. I recall one child, Eddie, a 9-year-old African American youngster possessed of great vitality and energy, who was particularly valuable in helping out with many tasks. These jobs included going around the city with an adult supervisor, finding recycled materials that could be used by teachers in developing arts programs, and then organizing them and even field-testing them back at the headquarters. In the context of this arts organization, Eddie was a definite asset.

A few months after this experience, I became involved in a special program through Lesley College in Cambridge, where I was getting my master's degree in special education. This project involved studying special education programs designed to help students who were having problems learning or behaving in regular classrooms in several Boston-area school districts. During one visit to a Cambridge resource room, I unexpectedly ran into Eddie. Eddie was a real problem in this classroom. He couldn't stay in his seat, wandered around the room, talked out of turn, and basically made the teacher's life miserable. Eddie seemed like a fish out of water. In the context of this school's special education program, Eddie was anything but an asset. In retrospect, he appeared to fit the definition of a child with attention deficit disorder (ADD).

A Growing National Phenomenon

Over the past 15 years, ADD has grown from a malady known only to a few cognitive researchers and special educators into a national phenomenon. Books on the subject have flooded the marketplace, as have special assessments, learning programs, residential schools, parent advocacy groups, clinical services, and medications to treat the "disorder." (The production of Ritalin or methylphenidate hydrochloride—the most common medication used to treat ADD—has increased 450% in the past four years, according to the Drug Enforcement Agency.) The disorder has solid support as a discrete medical problem from the Department of Education, the American Psychiatric Association, and many other agencies.

I'm troubled by the speed with which both the public and the professional community have embraced ADD. Thinking back to my experience with Eddie and the disparity that existed between Eddie in the arts organization and Eddie in the special education classroom, I wonder whether this "disorder" really exists in the child at all, or whether, more properly, it exists in the relationships that are present between the child and his or her environment. Unlike other medical disorders, such as diabetes or pneumonia, this is a disorder that pops up in one setting only to disappear in another. A physician mother of a child labeled ADD wrote to me not long ago about her frustration with this protean diagnosis: "I began pointing out to people that my child is capable of long periods of concentration when he is watching his favorite sci-fi video or examining the inner workings of a pin-tumbler lock. I notice that the next year's definition states that some kids with ADD are capable of normal attention in certain specific circumstances. Poof. A few thousand more kids instantly fall into the definition."

Disappearing Symptoms

There is in fact substantial evidence to suggest that children labeled ADD do not show symptoms of this disorder in several different real-life contexts. First, up to 80% of them don't appear to be ADD when in the physician's office. They also seem to behave normally in other unfamiliar settings where there is a one-to-one interaction with an adult (and this is especially true when the adult happens to be their father). Second, they appear to be indistinguishable from so-called normals when they are in classrooms or other learning environments where children can choose their own learning activities and pace themselves through those experiences. Third, they seem to perform quite normally when they are paid to do specific activities designed to assess attention. Fourth, and perhaps most significant, children labeled ADD behave and attend quite normally when they are involved in activities that interest them, that are novel in some way, or that involve high levels of stimulation. Finally, as many as 70% of these children reach adulthood only to discover that the ADD has apparently just gone away.

It's understandable, then, that prevalence figures for ADD vary widely—far more widely than the 3% to 5% figure that popular books and articles use as a standard. As Russell Barkley points out in his classic work on attention deficits, *Attention Deficit Hyperactivity Disorder: A Handbook for Diagnosis and Treatment*, the 3% to 5% figure "hinges on how one chooses to define ADHD, the population studied, the geographic locale of the survey, and even the degree of agreement required among parents, teachers and professionals. . . . Estimates vary between 1% and 20%."

In fact, estimates fluctuate even more than Barkley suggests. In one epidemiological survey conducted in England, only two children out of 2,199 were diagnosed as hyperactive (.09%). Conversely, in Israel, 28% of children were rated by teachers as hyperactive. And in an earlier study conducted in the U.S., teachers rated 49.7% of boys as restless, 43.5% of boys as having a "short attention span," and 43.5% of boys as "inattentive to what others say."

The Rating Game

These wildly divergent statistics call into question the assessments used to decide who is diagnosed as having ADD and who is not. Among the most frequently used tools for this purpose are behavior rating scales. These are typically checklists consisting of items that relate to the child's attention and behavior at home or at school. In one widely used assessment, teachers are asked to rate the child on a scale from 1 (almost never) to 5 (almost always) with regard to behavioral statements such as: "Fidgety (hands always busy)," "Restless (squirms in seat)," and "Follows a sequence of instructions." The problem with these scales is that they depend on subjective judgments by teachers and parents who may have a deep, and often subconscious, emotional investment in the outcome. After all, a diagnosis of ADD may lead to medication to keep a child compliant at home or may result in special education placement in the school to relieve a regular classroom teacher of having to teach a troublesome child.

Moreover, since these behavior rating scales depend on opinion rather than fact, there are no objective criteria through which to decide how much a child is demonstrating symptoms of ADD. What is the difference in terms of hard data, for example, between a child who scores a 5 on being

Whose Needs Are Being Met?

The rush to label schoolchildren as suffering from ADD or ADHD has reached nearly epidemic proportions. Currently, between 3% and 5% of U.S. students (1.35 million to 2.25 million children) have been diagnosed as having ADD. Is it time to investigate why this is happening? Perhaps there is more than one patient making the trip to the doctor's office: the child with the discipline problem and the child's parents. After all, there is no definitive test for the disorder and no agreed-upon etiology. There are no blood tests to be run, no x-rays to be taken. It would seem, at least on the surface, that people generally enjoy being told by their physician that they have a clean bill of health and have nothing wrong with them; why, then, do parents wish to come away with a diagnosis of ADD for their child?

The answer, of course, is that the diagnosis meets the needs of the parents more than it does those of the child. Almost at once, the parents feel relieved of some real or perceived pressures from educators, grandparents, and family friends. Having been unable to "control" the behavior of their children, they can now assign the control to Ritalin or some other drug. They are thus almost magically transformed into model parents. "I can't control you, son, but I have fulfilled my role as a parent by finding out what's 'wrong' with you." . . .

In addition, a parent may be less than effective in some areas of parenting. Denial of this shortcoming on the part of parents is natural and to be expected. These parents may seek the ADD diagnosis because it lets them off the hook, so to speak. It focuses attention on the child and on getting a prescription filled and thus demands no alteration of parents' behaviors or even any serious examination of them. The child now has a "medical condition" that has "nothing" to do with the child's upbringing. However, no parental introspection leads to no change in expectations or in conditions in the home. In this way, a diagnosis of ADD may not offset extremely negative conditions in a child's home that might best be served by the intervention of a social worker.

Richard W. Smelter et al., *Phi Delta Kappan*, February 1996.

fidgety and a child who scores a 4? Do the scores mean that the first child is one point more fidgety than the second? Of course not. The idea of assigning a number to a behavior trait raises the additional problem, addressed above, of context. The child may be a 5 on "fidgetiness" in some contexts (during worksheet time, for example) and a 1 at other times (during recess, during motivating activities, and at other highly stimulating times of the day). Who is to decide what the final number should be based on? If a teacher places more importance on workbook learning than on hands-on activities, such as building with blocks, the rating may be biased toward academic tasks, yet such an assessment would hardly paint an accurate picture of the child's total experience in school, let alone in life.

It's not surprising, then, to discover that there is often disagreement among parents, teachers, and professionals using these behavior rating scales as to who exactly is hyperactive or ADD. In one study, parent, teacher, and physician groups were asked to identify hyperactive children in a sample of 5,000 elementary school children. Approximately 5% were considered hyperactive by at least one of the groups, while only 1% were considered hyperactive by all three groups. In another study using a well-known behavior rating scale, mothers and fathers agreed that their children were hyperactive only about 32% of the time, and the correspondence between parent and teacher ratings was even worse: they agreed only about 13% of the time.

These behavior rating scales implicitly ask parents and teachers to compare a potential ADD child's attention and behavior to those of a "normal" child. But this raises the question, What is normal behavior? Do normal children fidget? Of course they do. Do normal children have trouble paying attention? Yes, under certain circumstances. Then exactly when does normal fidgeting turn into ADD fidgeting, and when does normal difficulty paying attention become ADD difficulty?

These questions have not been adequately addressed by professionals in the field, yet they remain pressing issues that seriously undermine the legitimacy of these behavior rating scales. Curiously, with all the focus being placed on children who score at the high end of the hyperactivity and distractibility continuum, virtually no one in the field talks about children who must statistically exist at the opposite end of the spectrum: children who are too focused, too compliant, too still, or too hypoactive. Why don't we have special classes, medications, and treatments for these children as well? . . .

The Stigma of ADD

Unfortunately, there seems to be little desire in the professional community to engage in dialogue about the reality of attention deficit disorder; its presence on the American educational scene seems to be a fait accompli. This is regrettable, since ADD is a psychiatric disorder, and millions of children and adults run the risk of stigmatization from the application of this label.

In 1991, when such major educational organizations as the National Education Association (NEA), the National Association of School Psychologists (NASP), and the National Association for the Advancement of Colored People (NAACP) successfully opposed the authorization by Congress of ADD as a legally handicapping condition, NEA spokesperson Debra DeLee wrote, "Establishing a new category ADD based on behavioral characteristics alone, such as overactivity, impulsiveness, and inattentiveness, increases the likelihood of inappropriate labeling for racial, ethnic, and linguistic minority students." And Peg Dawson, former NASP president, pointed out, "We don't think that a proliferation of labels is the best way to address the ADD issue. It's in the best interest of all children that we stop creating categories of exclusion and start responding to the needs of individual children." ADD nevertheless continues to gain ground as the label du jour in American education. It's time to stop and take stock of this "disorder" and decide whether it really exists or is instead more a manifestation of society's need to have such a disorder.

"Stimulants are the only treatment to date that normalizes the inattentive, impulsive, and restless behavior in ADHD children."

Ritalin Is Safe and Effective for Children with Attention Deficit Disorder

Russell A. Barkley, George J. DuPaul, and Anthony Costello

Stimulant drugs, such as Ritalin, are extremely effective in treating attention deficit disorder, maintain Russell A. Barkley, George J. DuPaul, and Anthony Costello in the following viewpoint. Many of the fears about using Ritalin—such as its dangerousness and addictiveness—are myths with no basis in fact, the authors contend. Moreover, since the drug's effects are extremely short-lasting, any potential ill-effects will wear off quickly, the authors assert. Barkley is the director of psychology and professor of psychiatry and neurology at the University of Massachusetts Medical Center (UMMC), and the author of several books on attention deficit disorder. DuPaul is a professor and coordinator of the Lehigh University School Psychology Program and has written numerous articles on attention deficit hyperactivity disorder. Costello is a child psychiatrist and the former director of the Division of Child and Adolescent Psychiatry at UMMC.

As you read, consider the following questions:

1. What was behind a dramatic decline in the use of Ritalin to treat ADD during the 1980s, according to the authors?
2. How does Ritalin affect a child's height and weight, as cited by the authors?

M edication is probably the most widely publicized, most hotly debated treatment for attention deficit hyperactivity disorder (ADHD). As a whole, the hundreds of studies conducted indicate that stimulants, antidepressants, and clonidine (a drug used to treat high blood pressure in many adults) can be of great help to those with ADHD. The stimulants, the drugs most commonly used, have been shown to be effective in improving behavior, academic work, and social adjustment in anywhere from 50% to 95% of children with ADHD. . . .

What *Not* to Believe

"Isn't Ritalin a dangerous drug? I've heard a lot of bad stories about this drug. Isn't it addictive? Won't it make my son more likely to take drugs later?'

Before you read on about how the stimulants work and what they may be able to do for your child, let's clear up a few misconceptions about these drugs:

Myth 1: Stimulant drugs are dangerous and should not be taken by any child. During the 1980s an inaccurate and, regrettably, successful media propaganda campaign against the use of stimulants, particularly Ritalin (methylphenidate), with children was waged by a fringe religious group, causing a dramatic decline in the prescribing of this medication in 1987–1989. Although the trend seems to have reversed since 1990, the use of stimulants with ADHD children continues to be controversial in the public's mind. Unfounded fear of these drugs is unfortunately perpetuated by some physicians' requirement that parents sign a consent form indicating that they have been informed about the medicines and their side effects and have agreed to have their child placed on one of them for treatment of the child's ADHD. *If your doctor asks you to sign such a form, don't assume it means the drugs are dangerous.* These forms arose only in response to the highly publicized threats of malpractice suits by the religious sect mentioned above, and some doctors still feel the need to protect themselves this way. . . .

Myth 2: Stimulants just cover up "the real problem" and do not deal directly with the root causes of the child's ADHD. Many parents come to us with this concern, but it is simply untrue.

The stimulants deal directly with the part of the brain that is underactive and gives rise to the outward symptoms of ADHD. In this sense, the stimulants are no different from using insulin for a child with diabetes. Unfortunately, like insulin, stimulants have only a temporary effect, which leads some people to believe they're masking the problem rather than helping it. Like a diabetic who needs insulin, your child may have to take stimulant medicine daily for a long time, but these drugs *are* a way of tackling the problem directly. *Stimulants are the only treatment to date that normalizes the inattentive, impulsive, and restless behavior in ADHD children.*

Myth 3: Stimulants make children "high" as other drugs do and are addictive. You may have heard that adults who take stimulants often have a sense of elevated mood, euphoria, or excessive well-being. While this does happen, it is not common, and in children it is rare. Some children do describe feeling "funny," "different," or dizzy. Others actually become a little bland in their mood, and a few even report feelings of sadness. These mood changes occur a few hours after the medicine is taken and occur more often among children treated with higher doses. In most children these changes are very minor.

Parents are often also quite concerned about the risk of addiction to stimulants and about an increased risk of abusing other drugs when the children become teenagers. There are no reported cases of addiction or serious drug dependence to date with these medications, and the several studies that have examined whether children on these drugs are more likely to abuse other substances as teenagers than those not taking them suggest that they are not.

Myth 4: Stimulant medications stunt children's growth, and their use is strictly limited by age. Some studies in the early 1970s seemed to suggest that children taking these medicines might be stunted in their height and weight gain. More recent and better studies have shown that this is not as much of a problem as was once thought. Your child's eventual adult height or skeletal size is not going to be affected by taking the medicine, and the effects on your child's weight are also likely to be minimal, resulting in a loss of one or two pounds during the initial year of treatment. Any weight lost should return by the second or later years of treatment. Keep in mind that children respond very differently to these medicines, some experiencing no weight change and others losing more than just a few pounds. Your child should be followed by your physician to make sure that this weight loss is not serious.

Myth 5: Stimulants can be used only by young children. Contrary to what you may have heard, stimulant medicines can be used throughout the life of the person with ADHD, not just during childhood. There was widespread concern in earlier decades that the stimulant medications could not be used once puberty started because they would no longer be effective. This was a fallacy, and we are now seeing a dramatic increase in the prescribing of these medications for teenagers having ADHD. We are also witnessing an increase in the use of these drugs with adults who have ADHD.

How the Stimulants Work

The stimulants are so named because of their ability to increase the level of activity or arousal of the brain. Then why don't they make people more hyperactive? Because it seems that the area of the brain they activate is responsible for inhibiting behavior and maintaining effort or attention to things. In a way, they increase the braking power of the brain over behavior. That seems to be why they are so helpful for those with ADHD.

The three most commonly recommended stimulants for ADHD are the drugs *d*-amphetamine (Dexedrine), methylphenidate (Ritalin), and pemoline (Cylert). Because caffeine (found in coffee, tea, soft drinks, and other foods) is a stimulant, some parents ask whether this drug or the beverages containing it will help their children with ADHD. Although there were some early reports in the popular press in the 1970s that caffeine might be useful, the scientific studies done on this subject have not borne this out. Therefore, we recommend that you consider only the three stimulant drugs just listed.

The stimulants work primarily by increasing the action of certain chemicals that occur naturally in the brain. The way the brain handles information is based on how these chemicals are produced in the brain cells (neurons). Although we don't know exactly which chemicals are influenced by the stimulants, we do know that two of them are dopamine and norepinephrine, both of which occur naturally throughout the brain but are concentrated very heavily in the frontal region, which we believe may be the site of the problem in ADHD. By increasing how much of these chemicals is available in the brain, the stimulants increase the action of these brain cells, which seem to be those most responsible for inhibiting our behavior and helping us stick to something we are doing.

Therefore it's not surprising that the hundreds of studies conducted on how these drugs change the behavior and learning of ADHD children show that between 70% and 90% of children treated with one of the stimulants improve in their behavior. Still, that leaves as many as 10% to 30% who show no positive response, some whose behavior is even made worse. So you can't assume that your child will necessarily benefit from medication, and we all must recognize that medication is no panacea for the problems that come with ADHD. There are some cases in which medication alone is enough or is the only practical way to address the concerns you and the teachers have about your child's ADHD. For most cases, though, the greatest benefit of stimulant therapy seems to be its ability to increase the effectiveness of psychological and educational treatments. Consequently, we normally recommend that when medication is indicated it be used as part of a combination of treatments, not as the sole form of therapy.

Behavior and Learning

What do the drugs do for behavior and emotions? Unquestionably the stimulants produce positive effects on sustained attention and persistence of effort to work. The medicines also reduce restlessness and gross motor activity. In many cases the child's attention to assigned classwork is so greatly improved that his or her behavior appears normal. Most children taking the medicine are far less impulsive and have fewer problems with aggression, noisiness, noncompliance, and disruptiveness—you can see why these medicines are so often recommended for children with ADHD.

How do the drugs change learning and academic performance? Numerous studies have been conducted on the effects of stimulants on children's intellect, memory, attention, and learning. They show that the stimulant medicines are very likely to improve a child's attention, impulse control, fine-motor coordination, and reaction time. Some children even show improvements in their short-term memory. When ADHD children have to do learning tasks, the medicine seems to help them perform more efficiently and in a more organized manner. No medicine can actually improve intelligence, but the stimulants increase your child's ability to show what he or she has already learned. In general, the drugs produce their greatest influence in situations that require children to restrict their behavior and concentrate on assigned tasks—situations like school.

You may have heard that once children stop taking the stimulants they will not be able to remember as easily what they learned while on it. Scientific studies of this problem have found it uncommon and too minor to be noticeable when it does occur.

Stimulant medications are not likely to improve your child's scores on school achievement tests, which measure the grade level or difficulty of the material children have learned. The medicines do, however, result in substantial increases in the amount of work a child is able to produce and in some cases increase the accuracy of the work as well.

Social Behavior

Do the medicines change social behavior? Yes. Treatment with stimulant medication has been found to reduce the intensity and improve the quality of social interactions between children with ADHD and their parents, teachers, and peers. Stimulants increase the children's ability to comply with a parent's commands and to maintain that compliance over time. The medicines also reduce behavior that competes with getting work done, such as inattention, distraction, and restlessness. In turn, parents and teachers respond by reducing their level of commands and the degree of supervision over the children.

They may also increase their praise and positive reactions

to the children. There has been some concern among professionals that these medicines may reduce a child's interest in socializing with others. Recent studies have not shown this to be a problem, but it may be possible if the child is taking a very high dose.

The degree of improvement differs among children, and each should be expected to have a unique response. We've seen no overall difference between boys and girls. We do expect to see greater improvement with higher doses, but your child's physician will have to try your child on several different doses before he or she discovers which one is best and may also have to try more than one drug.

No Other Treatment Compares

The safety and effectiveness of Ritalin and other stimulant drugs, including Dexedrine (dextroamphetamine) and Cylert (pemoline), have been established more firmly than any other treatments in the field of child and adolescent psychiatry. Literally scores of carefully conducted blind and double-blind controlled studies have repeatedly documented the improvement—often dramatic—in symptoms of attention deficit hyperactivity disorder (ADHD) following the use of stimulant medication, with Ritalin the most common choice. By contrast, no other treatment, including behavior modification, compares with stimulant medication in efficacy; in fact, no treatment besides these medications has had much success at all in treating ADHD.

Stimulant medication is so effective that a parent with a child diagnosed with ADHD should receive an explanation if the clinician's judgment is *not* to prescribe medication.

Jerry Wiener, *Priorities*, vol. 8 no. 3, 1996.

How long do the effects of the drugs last? Stimulants are almost always given orally when used for ADHD. They are swiftly absorbed into the bloodstream and cross into the brain quickly and easily. They are also eliminated from the body within 24 hours. This means you can rest assured that if your child has an undesirable reaction it will usually last only a few hours to a day. But it also means your child must take this medication several times a day, every day.

The medicines reach their peak in improving behavior

within one to three hours and may control behavior for three to six hours, but each child reacts somewhat differently, and each drug acts differently. Some changes in behavior are noticeable within 30 to 60 minutes after taking the medicine, again depending on which drug is being taken.

Both Ritalin and Dexedrine come in sustained-release preparations that usually begin to take effect after one to two hours, reach their peak influence after three to five hours, and may still have an effect after eight or more hours. However, these sustained-release forms may not be as powerful in their control over behavior, and again, all children react differently.

Cylert, or pemoline, works a little differently. It may start to have an effect after one to two hours, reach its peak in about two to four hours, and last for seven to nine hours or longer, but it does seem to build up in the body and may take a few days to a week before exerting its full effect.

Parents often ask whether children develop a tolerance to stimulants and whether they will need to have regular blood tests to monitor the amount of the drug in their bloodstream. Though some physicians have reported that a few children in their practice seemed to develop some tolerance (loss of effect) over a long period of use, research studies have not been able to document such an effect. Nor should the blood tests be of concern. The amount of drug in the bloodstream does not seem to be related to how well it works to control behavior, so there is no need for such tests.

> *"How has it come to pass that . . . millions of middle- and upper-middle class children are being legally drugged with a substance so similar to cocaine that . . . 'it takes a chemist to tell the difference?'"*

Ritalin Is Dangerous

Mary Eberstadt

Ritalin is a stimulant drug that is commonly prescribed to treat attention deficit disorder (ADD). In the following viewpoint, Mary Eberstadt points out that Ritalin shares many of the same characteristics as other drugs such as amphetamines, methamphetamine, and cocaine. In fact, Ritalin's physiological effects are almost indistinguishable from cocaine, she asserts. The number of children and adolescents who have abused Ritalin has increased dramatically, Eberstadt maintains. Therefore, she concludes, Ritalin is too dangerous to be used to drug typical childhood behaviors. Eberstadt is the consulting editor of *Policy Review*.

As you read, consider the following questions:
1. How has Ritalin produced a professional labor shortage, according to the *New York Times* as cited by Eberstadt?
2. How do lab animals respond to a choice between Ritalin and cocaine, according to Richard DeGrandpre as cited by the author?
3. What is a "drug holiday," as described by Eberstadt?

Excerpted from "Why Ritalin Rules," by Mary Eberstadt, *Policy Review*, April/May 1999. Reprinted with the permission of *Policy Review*.

There are stories that are mere signs of the times, and then there are stories so emblematic of a particular time and place that they demand to be designated cultural landmarks. Such a story was the *New York Times'* front-page report on January 18, 1999, appearing under the tame, even soporific headline, "For School Nurses, More Than Tending the Sick."

Ritalin Rules

"Ritalin, Ritalin, seizure drugs, Ritalin," in the words of its sing-song opening. "So goes the rhythm of noontime" for a typical school nurse in East Boston "as she trots her tray of brown plastic vials and paper water cups from class to class, dispensing pills into outstretched young palms." For this nurse, as for her counterparts in middle- and upper-middle class schools across the country, the day's routine is now driven by what the *Times* dubs "a ticklish question," to wit: "With the number of children across the country taking Ritalin estimated at well over three million, more than double the 1990 figure, who should be giving out the pills?"

"With nurses often serving more than one school at a time," the story goes on to explain, "the whole middle of the day can be taken up in a school-to-school scurry to dole out drugs." Massachusetts, for its part, has taken to having the nurse deputize "anyone from a principal to a secretary" to share the burden. In Florida, where the ratio of school nurses to students is particularly low, "many schools have clerical workers hand out the pills." So many pills, and so few professionals to go around. What else are the authorities to do?

Behold the uniquely American psychotropic universe, pediatrics zone—a place where "psychiatric medications in general have become more common in schools" and where, in particular, "Ritalin dominates." There are by now millions of stories in orbit here, and the particular one chosen by the *Times*—of how the drug has induced a professional labor shortage—is no doubt an estimable entry. But for the reader struck by some of the facts the *Times* mentions only in passing—for example, that Ritalin use more than doubled in the first half of the decade alone, that production has increased 700 percent since 1990, or that the number of schoolchildren taking the drug may now, by some estimates, be approaching the *4 million mark*—mere anecdote will only explain so much. . . .

Let's put the question bluntly: How has it come to pass that in *fin-de-siècle* America, where every child from pre-school onward can recite the "anti-drug" catechism by heart, millions of middle- and upper-middle class children are being legally drugged with a substance so similar to cocaine that, as one journalist accurately summarized the science, "it takes a chemist to tell the difference"?

What Is Methylphenidate?

The first thing that has made the Ritalin explosion possible is that methylphenidate, to use the generic term, is perhaps the most widely misunderstood drug in America today. Despite the fact that it is, as Lawrence Diller observes in *Running on Ritalin*, "the most intensively studied drug in pediatrics," most laymen remain under a misimpression both about the nature of the drug itself and about its pharmacological effects on children.

What most people believe about this drug is the same erroneous characterization that appeared elsewhere in the *Times* piece quoted earlier—that it is "a mild stimulant of the central nervous system that, for reasons not fully understood, often helps children who are chronically distractible, impulsive and hyperactive settle down and concentrate." The word "stimulant" here is at least medically accurate. "Mild," a more ambiguous judgment, depends partly on the dosage, and partly on whether the reader can imagine describing as "mild" *any* dosage of the drugs to which methylphenidate is closely related. These include dextroamphetamine (street name: "dexies"), methamphetamine (street name: "crystal meth"), and, of course, cocaine. But the chief substance of the *Times'* formulation here—that the reasons *why* Ritalin does what it does to children remain a medical mystery—is, as informed writers from all over the debate have long acknowledged, an enduring public myth.

"Methylphenidate," in the words of a 1995 DEA background paper on the drug, "is a central nervous system (CNS) stimulant and shares many of the pharmacological effects of amphetamine, methamphetamine, and cocaine." Further, it "produces behavioral, psychological, subjective, and reinforcing effects similar to those of d-amphetamine including increases in rating of euphoria, drug liking and activity, and decreases in sedation." For comparative purposes, that same DEA report includes a table listing the potential adverse physiological effects of both methylphenidate and dextroamphetamine; they are, as the table shows, nearly identical. To put the point conversely, as Richard DeGrandpre does in *Ritalin Nation* by quoting a 1995 report in the *Archives of General Psychiatry*, "Cocaine, which is one of the most reinforcing and addicting of the abused drugs, has pharmacological actions that are very similar to those of methylphenidate, which is now the most commonly prescribed psychotropic medicine for children in the U.S."

Ritalin Versus Cocaine

Such pharmacological similarities have been explored over the years in numerous studies. DeGrandpre reports that "lab animals given the choice to self-administer comparative doses of cocaine and Ritalin do not favor one over another" and that "a similar study showed monkeys would work in the same fashion for Ritalin as they would for cocaine." The DEA reports another finding—that methylphenidate is actually "chosen *over* cocaine in preference studies" of non-human primates (emphasis added). In *Driven to Distraction*, pro-Ritalin psychiatrists Hallowell and Ratey underline the interchangeable nature of methylphenidate and cocaine when they observe that "people with ADD feel focused when they take cocaine, *just as they do when they take Ritalin* (emphasis added)." Moreover, methylphenidate (like other stimulants) appears to increase tolerance for related drugs. Recent evidence indicates, for example, that when people accustomed to prescribed Ritalin turn to cocaine, they seek higher doses of it than do others. To summarize, again from the DEA report, "it is clear that methylphenidate substitutes for cocaine and d-amphetamine in a number of behavioral paradigms."

All of which is to say that Ritalin "works" on children in the same way that related stimulants work on adults—sharpening the short-term attention span when the drug kicks in and producing equally predictable valleys ("coming down," in the old street parlance; "rebounding," in Ritalinese) when the effect wears off. Just as predictably, children are subject to the same adverse effects as adults imbibing such drugs, with the two most common—appetite suppression and insomnia—being of particular concern. That is why, for example, handbooks on ADD will counsel parents to see their doctor if they feel their child is losing too much weight, and why some children who take methylphenidate are also prescribed sedatives to help them sleep. It is also why one of the more Orwellian phrases in the psychotropic universe, "drug holidays"—meaning scheduled times, typically on weekends or school vacations, when the dosage of methylphenidate is lowered or the drug temporarily withdrawn in order to keep its adverse effects in check—is now so common in the literature that it no longer even appears in quotations.

Just as, contrary to folklore, the adult and child physiologies respond in the same way to such drugs, so too do the physiologies of *all* people, regardless of whether they are diagnosed with ADD or hyperactivity. As Diller puts it, in a point echoed by many other sources, methylphenidate "potentially improves the performance of anyone—child or not, ADD-diagnosed or not." Writing in the *Public Interest* in 1997, psychologist Ken Livingston provided a similar summary of the research, citing "studies conducted during the mid seventies to early eighties by Judith Rapaport of the National Institute of Mental Health" which "clearly showed that stimulant drugs improve the performance of most people, regardless of whether they have a diagnosis of ADHD, on tasks requiring good attention." ("Indeed," he comments further in an obvious comparison, "this probably explains the high levels of 'self-medicating' around the world" in the form of "stimulants like caffeine and nicotine.")

Not Immune to Abuse

A third myth about methylphenidate is that it, alone among drugs of its kind, is immune to being abused. To the contrary: Abuse statistics have flourished alongside the boom in Ritalin prescription-writing. Though it is quite true that elementary schoolchildren are unlikely to ingest extra doses of the drug, which is presumably kept away from little hands, a very different pattern has emerged among teenagers and adults who have the manual dexterity to open prescription bottles and the wherewithal to chop up and snort their contents (a method that puts the drug into the bloodstream far faster than oral ingestion). For this group, statistics on the proliferating abuse of methylphenidate in schoolyards and on the street are dramatic.

Crystal Lite? Potential Adverse Effects of Ritalin and Dexies

Organic system affected	Methylphenidate	Dextroamphetamine
Cardiovascular	Palpitation	Palpitation
	Tachycardia	Tachycardia
	Increased blood pressure	Increased blood pressure
Central Nervous System	Excessive CNS stimulation	Excessive CNS stimulation
	Psychosis	Psychosis
	Dizziness	Dizziness
	Headache	Headache
	Insomnia	Insomnia
	Nervousness	Nervousness
	Irritability	Irritability
	Attacks of Gilles de la Tourette or other tic syndromes	Attacks of Gilles de la Tourette or other tic syndromes
Gastrointestinal	Anorexia	Anorexia
	Nausea	Nausea
	Vomiting	Vomiting
	Stomach pain	Stomach pain
	Dry mouth	Dry mouth
Endocrine/metabolic	Weight loss	Weight loss
	Growth suppression	Growth suppression

Mary Eberstadt, *Policy Review*, April/May 1999.

According to the DEA, for example, as early as 1994 Ritalin was the fastest-growing amphetamine being used "nonmedically" by high school seniors in Texas. In 1991, reports DeGrandpre in *Ritalin Nation*, "children between the ages of 10 and 14 years old were involved in only about 25 emergency room visits connected with Ritalin abuse. In 1995, just four years later, that number had climbed to more than 400 visits, which for this group was about the same number of visits as for cocaine." Not surprisingly, given these and other measures of methylphenidate's recreational appeal, criminal entrepreneurs have responded with interest to the drug's increased circulation. From 1990 to 1995, the DEA reports, there were about 2,000 thefts of methylphenidate, most of them night break-ins at pharmacies—meaning that the drug "ranks in the top 10 most frequently reported pharmaceutical drugs diverted from licensed handlers."

A Popular High on Campus

Because so many teenagers and college students have access to it, methylphenidate is particularly likely to be abused on school grounds. "The prescription drug Ritalin," reported *Newsweek* in 1995, "is now a popular high on campus—with some serious side effects." DeGrandpre notes that at his own college in Vermont, Ritalin was cited as the third-favorite drug to snort in a campus survey. He also runs, without comment, scores of individual abuse stories from newspapers across the country over several pages of his book. In *Running on Ritalin*, Diller cites several undercover narcotics agents who confirm that "Ritalin is cheaper and easier to purchase at playgrounds than on the street." He further reports one particularly hazardous fact about Ritalin abuse, namely that teenagers, especially, do not consider the drug to be anywhere near as dangerous as heroin or cocaine. To the contrary: "they think that since their younger brother takes it under a doctor's prescription, it must be safe."

In short, methylphenidate looks like an amphetamine, acts like an amphetamine, and is abused like an amphetamine. Perhaps not surprisingly, those who value its medicinal effects tend to explain the drug differently. To some, Ritalin is to children what Prozac and other psychotropic "mood brightening" drugs are to adults—a short-term fix for enhancing personality and performance. But the analogy is misleading. Prozac and its sisters are not stimulants with stimulant side effects; there is, ipso facto, no black market for drugs like these. Even more peculiar is the analogy favored by the advocates in CHADD: that "Just as a pair of glasses help the nearsighted person focus," as Hallowell and Ratey explain, "so can medication help the person with ADD see the world more clearly." But there is no black market for eyeglasses, either—nor loss of appetite, insomnia, "dysphoria" (an unexplained feeling of sadness that sometimes accompanies pediatric Ritalin-taking), nor even the faintest risk of toxic psychosis, to cite one of Ritalin's rare but dramatically chilling possible effects.

"Cognitive Steroids"

What is methylphenidate "really" like? Thomas Armstrong, writing in *The Myth of the ADD Child*, probably summarized the drug's appeal best. "Many middle- and upper-middle class parents," he observed then, "see Ritalin and related drugs almost as 'cognitive steroids' that can be used to help their kids focus on their schoolwork better than the next kid." Put this way, the attraction to Ritalin makes considerable sense. In some ways, one can argue, that after-lunch hit of low-dose methylphenidate is much like the big cup from Starbucks that millions of adults swig to get them through the day—but only in some ways. There is no dramatic upswing in hospital emergency room visits and pharmacy break-ins due to caffeine abuse; the brain being jolted awake in one case is that of an adult, and in the other that of a developing child; and, of course, the substance doing the jolting on all those children is not legally available and ubiquitous caffeine, but a substance that the DEA insists on calling a Schedule II drug, meaning that it is subject to the same controls, and for the same reasons of abuse potential, as related stimulants and other powerful drugs like morphine. . . .

Turning Childhood into a Disease

In the end, what has made the Ritalin outbreak not only possible but inevitable is the ongoing blessing of the American medical establishment—and not only that establishment. In a particularly enthusiastic account of the drug in a recent issue of the *New Yorker*, writer Malcolm Gladwell exults in the idea that "we are now extending to the young cognitive aids of a kind that used to be reserved exclusively for the old." He further suggests that, given expert estimates of the prevalence of ADD (up to 10 percent of the population, depending on the expert), if anything "too few" children are taking the drug. Surely all these experts have a point. Surely this country can do more, much more, to reduce fidgeting, squirming, talking excessively, interrupting, losing things, ignoring adults, and all those other pathologies of what used to be called childhood.

Periodical Bibliography

The following articles have been selected to supplement the diverse views presented in this chapter. Addresses are provided for periodicals not indexed in the *Readers' Guide to Periodical Literature*, the *Alternative Press Index*, the *Social Sciences Index*, or the *Index to Legal Periodicals and Books*.

Susan Brink	"Doing Ritalin Right," *U.S. News & World Report*, November 23, 1998.
Jane E. Brody	"Helping Children Avoid Depression," *New York Times*, December 9, 1997.
Richard Bromfield	"Fad or Disorder?" *American Health*, June 1996.
Patricia Chisholm	"The ADD Dilemma," *Maclean's*, March 11, 1996.
Howard Chua-Eoan	"Escaping from the Darkness," *Time*, May 31, 1999.
Malcom Gladwell	"Running from Ritalin," *New Yorker*, February 15, 1999.
Carey Goldberg	"For School Nurses, More Than Tending the Sick," *New York Times*, January 28, 1999.
Mark Nichols	"Genes or Parenting?" *Maclean's*, April 5, 1999.
Carly L. Price	"Is that All There Is?" *Common Boundary*, March/April 1998. Available from 5272 River Rd., #650, Bethesda, MD 20816.
Joyce Howard Price	"Experimenting on Children," *Insight*, November 23, 1998. Available from 3600 New York Ave. NE, Washington, DC 20002.
Jim Robbins	"Wired for Miracles," *New Age Journal*, March/April 1996. Available from 42 Pleasant St., Watertown, MA 02172.
Joannie M. Schrof	"Questioning Sybil," *U.S. News & World Report*, January 27, 1997.
Robert Sheppard	"Growing Up Hyperactive," *Maclean's*, September 7, 1998.
Elyse Tanouye	"Antidepressant Makers Study Kids' Market," *Wall Street Journal*, April 4, 1997.
Richard E. Vatz and Lee S. Weinberg	"How Accurate Is Media Coverage of Attention Deficit Disorder?" *USA Today*, July 1997.

CHAPTER 4

What Mental Health Treatments Are Beneficial?

Chapter Preface

Studies have shown that low levels of serotonin, a mood-regulating hormone, can cause depression. Antidepressants known as selective serotonin reuptake inhibitors (SSRIs) work by slowing down the reabsorption of serotonin into the neural system, thereby increasing the serotonin level in the brain. Thirty-five million people have used Prozac, the most prescribed SSRI, and its effects have been frequently praised. In a book about the experiences of SSRI users, Janet Thacker writes that since taking Prozac: "I smile, and I go out of my way to meet people and make friends." However, some critics wonder if Prozac has a dangerous effect on personality.

One incident that inspired debate was a 1989 mass shooting at a Kentucky factory. Joseph Wesbecker shot twenty co-workers, killing eight, before killing himself. Wesbecker had been taking Prozac for a month. Survivors and relatives of the victims sued Eli Lilly, the company that manufactures Prozac, on the grounds that the drug's side effects led to the shootings.

According to Gary Null, an investigative reporter, those side effects can include psychosis and extreme agitation. Peter Breggin, the author of *Talking Back to Prozac*, asserts that Prozac was inadequately tested and should not have been approved for sale. Null, noting Breggin's argument, observes: "Lilly knew beforehand that patients taking Prozac were having much higher suicide attempt rates than patients taking placebos or other drugs."

However not everyone agrees with those views. In his book *Listening to Prozac*, Peter D. Kramer writes that Wesbecker had long mental and emotional problems. Andrew Brown, a writer for the *Independent*, a London newspaper, also maintains that Prozac should not be blamed for Wesbecker's actions. According to Brown, "Human beings are not mere victims of their brain chemistry." In its lawsuit defense, Eli Lilly presented arguments similar to Kramer's and Brown's. Those arguments convinced the jury, which ruled in Eli Lilly's favor after five hours of deliberations.

SSRIs are not the only controversial treatment for mental illness. In the following chapter, the authors debate the efficacy of certain mental illness treatments.

| "Therapy for mental-health problems can have a substantial effect."

Psychotherapy Is Effective

Consumer Reports

In the following viewpoint, *Consumer Reports* argues that psychotherapy is an effective treatment for many mental illnesses. The magazine discusses a survey it conducted with its subscribers on their experiences with therapy. According to the survey, people who visit psychiatrists, psychologists, and social workers for at least six months are more likely to see improvements in their mental health than people who visit family doctors or attend fewer sessions. *Consumer Reports* is published by Consumers Union, a nonprofit, independent organization that provides impartial advice on products, health issues, and other consumer concerns.

As you read, consider the following questions:

1. According to a government survey cited by the magazine, what proportion of people suffering from a mental illness seek professional help?
2. Of the people whose emotional state was "very poor" prior to psychotherapy, what percentage said treatments "made things a lot better," as stated by *Consumer Reports*?
3. In the magazine's view, what are the three ways in which therapy improves mental health?

Excerpted from "Mental Health: Does Therapy Help?" editorial, *Consumer Reports*, November 1995. Copyright ©1995 by the Consumers Union of U.S., Inc., Yonkers, NY 10703-1057, a nonprofit organization. Reprinted with the permission of *Consumer Reports*, for educational purposes only. No commercial use or photocopying permitted. Subscription information available at www.ConsumerReports.org or by calling 1–800–234–1645.

Coping with a serious physical illness is hard enough. But if you're suffering from emotional or mental distress, it's particularly difficult to know where to get help. You may have some basic doubts about whether therapy will help at all. And even if you do decide to enter therapy, your health insurance may not cover it—or cover it well.

As a result, millions of Americans who might benefit from psychotherapy never even give it a try. More than 50 million American adults suffer from a mental or addictive disorder at any given time. But a government survey showed that fewer than one-third of them get professional help.

That's a shame. The results of a candid, in-depth survey of *Consumer Reports* subscribers—the largest survey ever to query people on mental-health care—provide convincing evidence that therapy can make an important difference. Four thousand of our readers who responded had sought help from a mental-health provider or a family doctor for psychological problems, or had joined a self-help group. The majority were highly satisfied with the care they received. Most had made strides toward resolving the problems that led to treatment, and almost all said life had become more manageable. This was true for all the conditions we asked about, even among the people who had felt the worst at the beginning.

Key Findings

• People were just as satisfied and reported similar progress whether they saw a social worker, psychologist, or psychiatrist. Those who consulted a marriage counselor, however, were somewhat less likely to feel they'd been helped.

• Readers who sought help from their family doctor tended to do well. But people who saw a mental-health specialist for more than six months did much better.

• Psychotherapy alone worked as well as psychotherapy combined with medication, like *Prozac* or *Xanax*. Most people who took drugs like those did feel they were helpful, but many people reported side effects.

• The longer people stayed in therapy, the more they improved. This suggests that limited mental-health insurance coverage, and the new trend in health plans—emphasizing short-term therapy—may be misguided.

- Most people who went to a self-help group were very satisfied with the experience and said they got better. People were especially grateful to Alcoholics Anonymous, and very loyal to that organization.

Information About the Survey

Our survey adds an important dimension to existing research in mental health. Most studies have started with people who have very specific, well-defined problems, who have been randomly assigned to a treatment or control group, and who have received carefully scripted therapy. Such studies have shown which techniques can help which problems, but they aren't a realistic reflection of most patients' experiences.

Our survey, in contrast, is a unique look at what happens in real life, where problems are diverse and less well-defined, and where some therapists try one technique after another until something works. The success of therapy under these real-life conditions has never before been well studied, says Martin Seligman, former director of clinical training in psychology at the University of Pennsylvania and past president of the American Psychological Association's division of clinical psychology.

Seligman, a consultant to our project, believes our readers' experiences send "a message of hope" for other people dealing with emotional problems.

Like other surveys, ours has several built-in limitations. Few of the people responding had a chronic, disabling condition such as schizophrenia or manic depression. We asked readers about their past experiences, which can be less reliable than asking about the present. We may have sampled an unusually large number of people in long-term treatment. Finally, our data comes from the readers' own perceptions, rather than from a clinician's assessment. However, other studies have shown that such self-reports frequently agree with professionals' clinical judgments.

The Average Patient

In our 1994 Annual Questionnaire, we asked readers about their experiences with emotional problems and their encounters with health-care providers and groups during the years 1991 to 1994. Like the average American outpatient client, the 4000 readers who said they had sought professional help were mostly well educated. Their median age was 46, and about half were women. However, they may be more amenable to therapy than most.

Many who went to a mental-health specialist were in considerable pain at the time they entered treatment. Forty-three percent said their emotional state was either very poor ("I barely managed to deal with things") or fairly poor ("Life was usually pretty tough").

Their reasons for seeking therapy included several classic emotional illnesses: depression, anxiety, panic, and phobias. Among the other reasons our readers sought therapy: marital or sexual problems, frequent low moods, problems with children, problems with jobs, grief, stress-related ailments, and alcohol or drug problems.

Therapy Works

Our survey showed that therapy for mental-health problems can have a substantial effect. Forty-four percent of people whose emotional state was "very poor" at the start of treatment said they now feel good. Another 43 percent who started out "fairly poor" also improved significantly, though somewhat less. Of course, some people probably would have gotten better without treatment, but the vast majority specifically said that therapy helped.

Most people reported they were helped with the specific problems that brought them to therapy, even when those problems were quite severe. Of those who started out "very poor," 54 percent said treatment "made things a lot better," while another one-third said it helped their problems to some extent. The same pattern of improvement held for just about every condition.

Overall, almost everyone who sought help experienced some relief—improvements that made them less troubled and their lives more pleasant. People who started out feeling the worst reported the most progress. Among people no longer in treatment, two-thirds said they'd left because their problems had been resolved or were easier to deal with.

Rating the Therapists

In the vast field of mental health, psychiatrists, psychologists, and clinical social workers have long fought for turf. Only psychiatrists, who are medical doctors, can prescribe drugs and have the training to detect medical problems that can affect a person's mental state. Otherwise, each of these professionals is trained to understand human behavior, to recognize problems, and to provide therapy.

Historically, social workers have been the underdogs and have had to fight for state laws requiring insurance companies to cover their services. But many of today's budget-minded insurers *favor* social workers—and psychiatric nurses—because they offer relatively low-cost services.

Therapy Can Be Very Helpful

Almost everyone got some relief from the problems that brought them to a therapist, no matter how poorly they felt at the start.

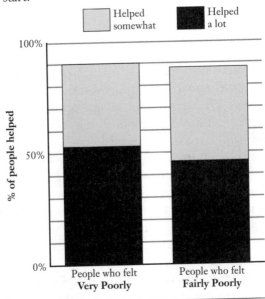

In our survey, almost three-quarters of those seeking professional help went to a mental-health specialist. Their experiences suggest that any of these therapists can be very helpful. Psychiatrists, psychologists, and social workers received equally high marks and were praised for being supportive, insightful, and easy to confide in. That remained true even when we statistically controlled for the seriousness and type of the problem and the length of treatment

Those who went to marriage counselors didn't do quite as well, and gave their counselors lower grades for competence. One reason may be that working with a fractured couple is difficult. Also, almost anyone can hang out a shingle as a marriage counselor. In some states the title "marriage and family therapist" is restricted to those with appropriate training. But anyone can use other words to say they *do* marriage therapy, and in most places the title "marriage counselor" is up for grabs.

Family Doctors Are Less Effective

Many people are more comfortable taking their problems to their family doctor than to a psychologist or psychiatrist. That may work well for some people, but our data suggest that many would be better off with a psychotherapist.

Readers who exclusively saw their family doctor for emotional problems—about 14 percent of those in our survey—had a very different experience from those who consulted a mental-health specialist. Treatment tended to be shorter; more than half of those whose care was complete had been treated for less than two months. People who went to family doctors were much more likely to get psychiatric drugs—83 percent of them did, compared with 20 percent of those who went to mental-health specialists. And almost half the people whose doctors gave them drugs received medication without the benefit of much counseling.

The people who relied on their family doctors for help were less distraught at the outset than those who saw mental-health providers; people with severe emotional problems apparently get themselves to a specialist. Even so, only half were highly satisfied with their family doctor's treatment (compared with 62 percent who were highly satisfied with their mental-health provider). A significant minority felt their doctor had neither the time nor temperament to address emotional issues. In general, family doctors did help people get back on their feet—but longer treatment with a specialist was more effective.

However, if you begin treatment with your family doctor, that's where you're likely to stay. Family doctors referred their patients to a mental-health specialist in only one out of four cases, even when psychotherapy might have made a big difference. Only half of those who were severely distressed were sent on, and 60 percent of patients with panic disorder or phobias were never referred, even though specific therapies are known to work for those problems.

Other research has shown that many family doctors have a poor track record when it comes to mental health. They fail to diagnose some 50 to 80 percent of psychological problems, and sometimes prescribe psychiatric drugs for too short a time or at doses too low to work. . . .

Guidelines for Receiving Treatment

When a person needs psychotherapy, how much do they need? That has become a critical question—both for clinicians and for the insurers that pay for therapy. And it's a hard one to answer.

Nationally, most people who get therapy go for a relatively short time—an average of four to eight sessions. It's not clear, however, whether people stop going because they have been helped enough, because they don't think the therapy is working, or because they've run out of money. Controlled studies of specific kinds of therapy usually cover only 12 to 20 visits. While brief therapy often helps, there's no way to tell from such studies whether 30 or 40 sessions, or even more, would be even more effective.

For the people in our survey, longer psychotherapy was associated with better outcomes. Among people who entered therapy with similar levels of emotional distress, those who stayed in treatment for more than six months reported greater gains than those who left earlier. Our data suggests that for many people, even a year's worth of therapy with a mental-health specialist may be very worthwhile. People who stayed in treatment for more than two years reported the best outcomes of all. However, these people tended to have started out with more serious problems.

We also found that people got better in three distinct ways, and that all three kinds of improvement increased with additional treatment. First, therapy eased the problems that brought people to treatment. Second, it helped them to function better, improving their ability to relate well to others, to be productive at work, and to cope with everyday stress. And it enhanced what can be called "personal growth." People in therapy had more confidence and self-esteem, understood themselves better, and enjoyed life more.

Despite the potential benefit of long-term therapy, many insurance plans limit mental-health coverage to "medically necessary" services—which typically means short-term treatment aimed at symptom relief. If you want to stay in therapy longer, you may have to pay for it yourself.

Our findings complement work by psychologist Kenneth Howard of Northwestern University. By following the progress of 854 psychotherapy patients, Howard and his associates found that recovery followed a "dose-response" curve, with the greatest response occurring early on. On average, 50 percent of people recovered after 11 weekly therapy sessions, and 75 percent got better after about a year.

Emotional distress may not always require professional help. But when problems threaten to become overwhelming or interfere with everyday life, there's no need to feel defeated.

Our survey shows there's real help available from every quarter—family doctors, psychotherapists, and self-help groups. Both talk therapy and medication, when warranted, can bring relief to people with a wide range of problems and deep despair.

"Most of the psychotherapy research over the years has reported an effectiveness level no better than that achieved by placebo conditions."

Psychotherapy Is Harmful and Ineffective

Al Siebert

Psychotherapy does not cure mental illness and can cause further damage to a patient, argues Al Siebert in the following viewpoint. He asserts that psychotherapy is no more effective than placebo treatments, which soothe the patient but do not actually treat the disorder in question. In addition, Siebert maintains that psychiatrists and psychologists cause considerable damage to patients and families by misdiagnosing people as mentally ill, but that the doctors at fault rarely face legal repercussions. Siebert is a psychologist and the author of *The Survivor Personality*.

As you read, consider the following questions:
1. What does Siebert cite as evidence that mental patients have been harmed in psychiatric facilities?
2. According to the author, why does psychotherapy carry a low risk for a malpractice lawsuit?
3. In Siebert's view, what are two safety issues that must be addressed?

Excerpted from "What If Psychotherapies Had to Meet FDA Standards for Effectiveness, Safety, and Appropriateness?" by Al Siebert, available at www.webcom.com/thrive/schizo/articles/fda.html. Reprinted with permission from the author.

If a criterion and policy for efficacy similar to that used by the FDA for drugs is established for new and already existing psychotherapies, then most psychotherapy as currently practiced would have to be banned by the regulating agency. Here's why:

> Title 21, Chapter One, Section 312.1 of Food and Drug Administration policies, establishes that a plan for clinical trials using treated subjects and control subjects must show that the effects and results obtained must be attributable to the drug under investigation. As explained by FDA Associate Commissioner Pines (1981), "the investigator must have a basis for determining that the drug is causing the desired effect, rather than other variables, or chance."

Thus for a new drug to be approved or an old drug allowed to continue to be marketed, there must be convincing evidence that the same result could not be obtained by any other means. Such efficacy is typically established in double-blind experiments in which neither the physicians nor the patients know if the medication given is the real drug or a placebo. In other words, efficacy is established by proving that the drug gets significantly better results than a placebo.

Psychotherapy and Placebos

Hence the problem for psychotherapists if an efficacy standard similar to that developed by the FDA is adopted. Most of the psychotherapy research over the years has reported an effectiveness level no better than that achieved by placebo conditions. In fact, [Mary Lee] Smith, [Gene V.] Glass, and [Thomas I.] Miller, in their widely publicized book about psychotherapy being beneficial [*The Benefits of Psychotherapy*], include "Placebo Treatment" as one type of psychotherapy. Although Smith, et al. state that placebo treatments are slightly less effective than specific psychotherapies, [Leslie] Prioleau, [Martha] Murdock, and [Nathan] Brody report that in the Smith et al. meta-analysis there were only 32 studies in which psychotherapy with real patients was compared with placebo treatment, and that in these 32 studies "there is no evidence that the benefits of psychotherapy are greater than those of placebo treatment."

The basic issue here is that the professional standard for many psychotherapists is to accept an efficacy criterion which is no better than the placebo effect. If an efficacy standard similar to what the FDA has established for drugs is adopted, in which both new and existing treatments must be proven to have more effect than placebo treatment, what will be the consequences for psychotherapists?

Some Therapy Is Harmful

Research reports into the outcomes of psychotherapy and psychiatric treatment seldom draw attention to the harm done to some patients by their therapists. Smith, et al., for example, spent two years intensively studying 475 published reports of psychotherapy outcomes and claim that "there is scant evidence of negative or deterioration effects of psychotherapy." Anyone who has worked in clinical settings, however, knows that some patients are harmed by psychotherapeutic efforts.

[Carl R.] Rogers, [Eugene T.] Gendlin, [Donald J.] Kiesler, and [Charles B.] Truax specifically state, in reporting the findings of the Wisconsin psychotherapy study, that "therapy must . . . bear the onus of contributing to the deterioration of some of the patients. If this is the case, then this study provides evidence of the harmful as well as the salutary effects of psychotherapy. Therapy, it seems, should no longer be viewed as either helpful or safely benign."

Psychiatrist Manfred Bellak concluded toward the end of his career that "what used to be considered pathogenic 'schizophrenic regression' is probably largely 'iatrogenic.' Patients were isolated from the families and communities in which they lived, held in wards with perceptual isolation and sensory deprivation and suffered from disuse atrophy of their ego functions. A sense of hopelessness was fostered in institutions run in a poor and dictatorial fashion by an ill-trained staff. . . . Acts of sadism were tolerated, if not encouraged. Visiting privileges were limited. Telephone privileges rare, and all mail was censored."

Evidence that mental patients have been seriously harmed in psychiatric facilities and that a serious social injustice exists is seen in the spontaneous formation of dozens of volunteer groups organized to combat, stop, and change the existing mental health system. These groups have formed a loose national network, hold a national convention each year, and organize demonstrations at the American Psychiatric Association conventions.

Libraries and book stores contain many accounts by ex-mental patients attempting to tell the world about their distressing experiences. Judi Chamberlin, for example, writes "Many ex-patients are angry, and our anger stems from the neglect, indifference, dehumanization, and outright brutality we have seen and experienced at the hands of the mental health system. Our distrust of professionals is not irrational hostility, but is the direct result of their treatment of us in the past. We have been belittled, ignored, and lied to. We have no reason to trust professionals, and many reasons to fear them."

No Legal Repercussions

The illusion that psychotherapy is safe stems in part from the low risk psychotherapists have about malpractice lawsuits. The risk of a malpractice lawsuit is so low that many psychotherapists do not even bother with such insurance. Those who do take out malpractice learn that they qualify for the very lowest rates.

Are the risks and rates low because psychotherapy is safe? No.

The risks and rates are low because there is not one case in the history of United States law in which a psychiatrist or psychologist was found to have made a mistake in diagnosing a person as mentally ill and required to pay damages for harm and suffering caused by the mistake. This is an extraordinary statistic considering the fact that for many decades approximately one-half of all the hospital beds in the nation have been occupied by persons diagnosed as mentally ill.

Why has there never been one adjudicated error in the diagnosis of mental illness in the entire history of psychiatry and clinical psychology? Because the standard of practice is to regard every human as mentally ill to some extent. This way of thinking is derived from Sigmund Freud who believed that every human has some psychopathology. Freud declared that in reality no one is "normal." He called "normality in general an ideal fiction" and said that "every normal person is only approximately normal: his ego resembles that of the psychotic in one point or another, in a greater or lesser degree. . . ."

Too Many Therapies

Owing, perhaps, to the historical connection between psychotherapy and the medical model, most theory and practice since the time of Freud have been focused on identifying the underlying causes of mental suffering. Indeed, as distinguished philosopher Paul Watzlawick noted, the assumption has been "that the discovery of the real causes of the [client's] problem is a *conditio sine qua non* for change."

The idea, of course, is that knowing the underlying cause of a particular problem would lead, as so often has been the case in physical medicine, to the identification and/or development of effective treatments. Over time, various causes have been advanced by various psychotherapy theories. For example, with their emphasis on early life experiences, psychodynamic theories have traditionally located the cause of mental health problems in childhood. Cognitive therapies, on the other hand, with their emphasis on thought processes, identify the cause of suffering as problematic or dysfunctional patterns of thinking.

Unfortunately, in spite of nearly 100 years of hypothesizing, no consensus exists among clinicians, theoreticians, or researchers regarding the root (and presumed real) causes of most problems in psychotherapy. Rather, it seems that the etiology of an individual's problem depends, for the most part, on the particular therapist that the client happens to see or the etiological theory that is in vogue at the time treatment is conducted.

Scott D. Miller, Mark A. Hubble, and Barry L. Duncan, *Professional Counselor*, February 1997.

Two psychiatrists highly influential in the development of American psychiatry and the development of laws governing commitment procedures, William and Karl Menninger, were strongly Freudian. They echoed Freud's views that every person is at one time or another mentally ill.

Everyone Is Considered Mentally Ill

A scientific study which helped prove how extensively mental illness is believed to be present in the population is the

Midtown Manhattan Study. This study reports the results of an extensive research project designed to assess the mental health of Americans. Experienced researchers using good sampling techniques had 1660 adults (ages 20-59) interviewed in their homes and evaluated by psychiatrists.

Table 1
Home Survey Sample (Age 20–59)

18.5%	Well
36.3%	Mild Symptom Formation
21.8%	Moderate Symptom Formation
13.2%	Marked Symptom Formation
7.5%	Severe Symptom Formation
2.7%	Incapacitated

About the people in the "Well" category, the authors of the project state, "In Table 1 we see that roughly 1 in 5 (18.5%) respondents were viewed by the team psychiatrists as free of other than inconsequential symptoms and can be regarded as essentially Well." Thus the authors of this scientific study, using accepted research techniques, did not find one person to be without mental illness.

No psychiatric articles disagreed with the study's findings nor has any research published since then negated any of the findings. [Patrick] DeLeon, [Gary] VandenBos, and [Nicholas] Cummings, for example, have observed that "mental health providers can present a rationale for why any person could, or should, be seen in psychotherapy."

In regard to the criterion of safety, therefore, there are two issues which must be addressed:

Why should Congress mandate funding for psychotherapy for persons covered under Medicare and in Health Maintenance Organizations when the professional standards of psychotherapists can justify therapy for every person covered?

A more compelling issue, however, is about patients' rights in cases of malpractice. How can a patient ever collect damages for harm stemming from a wrong diagnosis when the current professional standards are that no professional ever makes a mistake in diagnosing a person as mentally ill?

*"[Electroconvulsive therapy] is both effective
and safe."*

Electroconvulsive Therapy Is an Effective Treatment for Schizophrenia and Depression

Rael Jean Isaac

In the following viewpoint, Rael Jean Isaac asserts that electroconvulsive therapy (ECT)—in which pulsed electricity is sent through electrodes that have been placed on a patient's head, inducing a brief seizure—is a safe and effective treatment for schizophrenics and depressives. According to Isaac, ECT has few side effects other than temporary memory loss and is safer than antidepressants. However, Isaac notes that the misrepresentation of ECT by its opponents and the media has greatly restricted its accessibility. Isaac is the co-author of *Madness in the Streets: How Psychiatry and the Law Abandoned the Mentally Ill*.

As you read, consider the following questions:

1. According to Richard Wiener, as cited by Isaac, what is the likelihood that ECT is more effective than anti-depressants in the treatment of depression?
2. In the author's opinion, ECT is advantageous for which patients?
3. According to Isaac, why is memory loss considered to be ECT's most frightening side effect?

Excerpted from "Electroconvulsive Therapy: Maligned and Misunderstood," by Rael Jean Isaac, *Priorities for Health*, vol. 11, no. 1, 1999. Reprinted with permission from *Priorities for Health*, a publication of the American Council on Science and Health, 1995 Broadway, 2nd floor, New York, NY 10023-5860. Additional information available at www.acsh.org.

Noted psychiatry professor Trevor Price, M.D., has called electroconvulsive therapy (ECT) "one of the most dramatically effective and safest treatments in psychiatry, if not all of medicine."

Basic Facts About ECT

The most crucial element of ECT (lay terms for which include "electroshock" and "electroshock therapy") is not electricity but the seizure the electricity induces. Earlier forms of shock treatment induced a seizure in other ways. Insulin, for example, was used to effect a brain seizure by reducing blood sugar. The chemical metrazol was also used as a seizure inducer, but such treatment was extremely unpleasant for patients (one called it a roller coaster to hell). In modern forms of ECT, an anesthetic and a muscle relaxant are given before electricity is applied.

Traditional ECT is bilateral. Electrodes are placed on both sides of the head, and pulsed electricity is sent through them that induces an approximately 60-second seizure in the brain. Typically, the ECT patient undergoes 6 to 12 treatments over two to four weeks. Researchers have found that patients liken the experience to a dental visit. In a survey, Dr. Helen Pettinati found that 98 percent of patients who had undergone ECT for depression would consent to another round if they re-experienced the illness.

ECT was first developed in Italy in 1938, by neurologist Ugo Cerletti and his assistant Lucio Bini. The first ECT patient was an unidentified catatonic man, around 40 years old, who had been found in the Milan train station without a ticket, uttering gibberish. For several decades thereafter, ECT was used primarily against schizophrenia. Since the 1970s it has been used primarily against depression; and, indeed, it is often referred to as the gold standard for treating psychotic (delusional) depression.

Duke University psychiatry professor Richard Wiener, M.D., an authority on ECT, has stated that, according to meta-analytic studies (studies whose conclusions stem from statistically combining data from many studies), the likelihood that ECT is more effective against depression than are antidepressants is 99.99 percent. (A probability of 95 percent is usually considered adequate for deciding whether one modality is better than another.) In 1987 the American Psychiatric Association (APA) appointed Wiener to chair a task force on ECT. The task force concluded that ECT was effective not only against depression but also against mania (a condition marked by overstimulation and a lack of judgment and self-control), bipolar disorder (manic depression), and some types of schizophrenia. The APA endorsed its conclusions in 1990.

Treating Schizophrenia

Schizophrenia remains the illness against which the effectiveness of ECT has been least established. Various studies have shown that ECT is rarely effective against chronic schizophrenia characterized by slow development—what psychiatrists call "insidious onset." But ECT is often very effective when it is administered early in cases of what psychiatrists call "acute onset schizophrenia." Indeed, according to Matthew Rudorfer, M.D., chief of the Services and Intervention Research Branch of the National Institute of Mental Health (NIMH), Eli Robbins, his mentor and one of the fathers of biological psychiatry, believed that ECT should be tried on all young psychotic patients because it would at best spare them a long future of dysfunction and at least delay their needing neuroleptics and undergoing the debilitating side effects of such drugs. Richard Wyatt, M.D., chief of the NIMH's Neuropsychiatry Branch, has reported that, in his appraisal of studies conducted in the 1950s, he found that patients who had been treated with ECT after their first psychotic break had responded better in the long run than had patients who'd been treated with neuroleptics (then a new class of drugs). Regrettably, because of controversy in the public arena over ECT, physicians almost never administer it to young psychotic patients.

Psychiatrists have found that the more a case of depressive illness resembles schizophrenia (with delusions), and the more a case of schizophrenia resembles a depressive illness (with such "vegetative" symptoms as motor retardation and sleep disturbance), the likelier that the patient will benefit from ECT. One of England's top experts on ECT, Pamela

Taylor of London's Institute of Psychiatry, has asserted that, while there is general recognition that patients suffering from depression accompanied by delusions respond especially well to ECT, "It's also quite clear from the schizophrenia work . . . that it is actually the delusional and the more frankly psychotic symptoms that respond."

ECT is both effective and safe—safer than antidepressants, whose use is much more extensive. Thus, it is advantageous not only for patients who have not responded to medications or are considered suicidal (ECT works much more quickly than medications) but also for patients for whom the side effects of antidepressants would be inordinately hazardous, especially elderly persons and pregnant women.

ECT and Memory Loss

ECT has only one important adverse side effect: memory impairment. Everyone who undergoes an ECT series loses some memories of events of months immediately preceding and following the treatment; the more treatments, the larger the memory loss. The greatest impact on memory concerns the prior six months and the subsequent two months, but otherwise the effect is tremendously variable. In *Holiday of Darkness: A Psychologist's Personal Journey Out of Depression* (1982 and 1990), an account of bouts of severe depression and recovery through ECT, Canadian psychology professor Norman Endler declared: "Neither the depression nor the ECT produced any memory loss. I had a super memory before; I still have one now." On the other hand, a small proportion of ECT patients (the APA has estimated 1 in 200) complain of serious, long-term memory loss. Most of the memories that ECT affects are "autobiographical"—memories of events in which the patient participated—particularly memories of experiences that were approximately contemporary with the treatments.

The effect of ECT on memory has been studied extensively, and in most objective tests—such as tests of individuals' ability to recollect television shows or events reported in the news—ECT patients have performed as well as the controls performed. In his 1997 book *Electroconvulsive Ther-*

apy—the third edition of the standard work on the subject—Richard Abrams, M.D., states that, according to the memory studies, ECT: (a) does not permanently affect the ability to learn and remember; and (b) does not affect other cognitive abilities, such as visual-motor skills and the capacity for applying knowledge.

ECT and Patient Consent

When the physician has determined that clinical indications justify the administration of ECT, the law requires, and medical ethics demand, that the patient's freedom to accept or refuse the treatment be fully honored. An ongoing consultative process should take place. In this process, the physician must make clear to the patient the nature of the options available and the fact that the patient is entitled to choose among those options.

No uniform "shopping list" can be drawn up regarding the matters that should be discussed by patient and physician to assure a fully informed consent. They should discuss the character of the procedure, its possible risks and benefits (including full acknowledgement of posttreatment confusion, memory dysfunction, and other attendant uncertainties), and the alternative treatment options (including the option of no treatment at all). Special individual needs may also be relevant to some patients, for example, a personal situation that requires rapid remission to facilitate return to work and to reduce family disruption. In all matters, the patient should not be inundated with technical detail; the technical issues should be translated into terms meaningful and accessible to the patient.

National Institute of Mental Health Consensus Study, "Electroconvulsive Therapy," http://www.schizophrenia.com/ami/meds/ect.html.

Memory impairment from unilateral ECT—the form of ECT in which both electrodes are placed on one side of the head (usually the right side)—is much less than that from bilateral ECT. Clinicians have found, however, that unilateral ECT is often much less effective than bilateral ECT. According to surveys, the proportion of clinicians who first administer ECT as unilateral ECT has risen sharply since the 1970s, but in a 1993 study it was found that 52 percent of ECT providers used only bilateral ECT.

The mechanism whereby ECT affects memory is uncertain. Some researchers have hypothesized that ECT temporarily interrupts protein synthesis and thereby prevents consolidation of what was recently learned and/or that it alters neurotransmitter systems related to memory.

As a whole, the many studies to determine whether ECT structurally damages the brain have not substantiated the hypothesis that ECT does such harm. Findings from animal experiments of the 1940s suggested that ECT destroys brain cells, but these experiments were faulty: The findings resulted from improper tissue-preservation methods. Findings from comparable studies in which better techniques were used suggest no brain-cell destruction. In 1994 *The American Journal of Psychiatry* featured "Does ECT Alter Brain Structure?" New York State Psychiatric Institute professor D.P. Devanand, M.D., was the lead author of this survey, the most comprehensive to date, of all research relevant to the issue of whether ECT structurally damages the brain. Devanand and his associates concluded that there was "no evidence of structural brain damage as a result of ECT."

Why ECT Is Feared

Why, then, is the treatment so controversial?

• Because memories and self-identity are inseparable, even a time-limited loss of memories—ECT's only serious side effect—is more frightening than other, even more harmful, side effects, such as those of many drugs.

• "Convulsions," "shock," and other parts of the language of ECT conjure frightening images. To many individuals, the idea of passing electricity through the brain suggests the electric chair—the punishment society reserves for its most heinous murderers.

• Hollywood has embedded in the public consciousness frightful notions of ECT. In the big Oscar-winner *One Flew Over the Cuckoo's Nest* (1975), for example, it is portrayed as torture—particularly as a means of subduing the nonconformist hero, R.P. McMurphy (played by Jack Nicholson), who is not mentally ill at all. Although modern ECT—marked by anesthesia and the use of muscle relaxants—had been standard for more than a decade when filming began, the movie depicts old-fashioned ECT, long in disuse, with McMurphy writhing and convulsing.

• In the initial enthusiasm for ECT, which in the pre-neurolepic era was rightly considered a breakthrough treatment, it was used too aggressively. Sometimes it was used misguidedly. In the late 1950s Ewen Cameron, M.D., and associates researched the effects of what they termed "de-patterning treatment" on patients with chronic paranoid schizophrenia. This featured administering ECT up to 60 times to each patient, 12 times a day. The patients became incontinent and profoundly disoriented, and many of them suffered pronounced memory loss. Nevertheless, some hospitals adopted the method. A private hospital in Connecticut used it on the basis of the erroneous psychoanalytic theory that regressing a patient to an infantile state through ECT enables restructuring his or her personality.

• Scientologists, who aspire "to take over the field of mental health by the year 2000," and a small group of vociferous former ECT patients (both abetted by a few maverick psychiatrists) have continually attacked ECT—on daytime talk shows, in legislative forums, and in various other settings.

ECT Is Too Inaccessible

Mental illness impairs insight, and it is likely that former ECT patients who have become opposed to ECT have forgotten how sick they were before treatment—though their families may remember it too clearly. For example, Linda Andre, a leader in the anti-ECT movement, has said that her parents consider ECT the best thing since the introduction of sliced bread.

Because of the anti-ECT movement and the media's misrepresentation of the treatment, ECT is far less available than it should be. It is offered almost entirely in the private sector, mostly by university hospitals. The incidence of ECT administration is unknown. According to educated guesses by experts in the field, 30,000 to 100,000 patients a year undergo ECT. It is clear, however, that ECT is largely inaccessible in the public sector, on which most of the sickest (and poorest) patients depend and where political influence is most easily brought to bear. State and municipal hospitals rarely offer ECT. Veterans Administration hospitals also seldom offer the treatment, even though a very high percentage of their patients suffer from depression—the illness most remediable by ECT. In 1995 *The American Journal of Psychiatry* conveyed a disturbing finding from an epidemiological survey conducted by Harvard Medical School professor Robert Dorwart, M.D., and colleagues: In more than a third of the metropolitan areas of the United States, ECT had not been administered at all during the month the survey covered.

Efforts are ongoing to abolish ECT by legislation or regulation. . . . In 1974 the California legislature made getting ECT in that state almost impossible, and in 1983 the city of Berkeley outlawed it entirely. In both instances courts overturned the laws. Today, Texas is in the vanguard of the anti-ECT movement, with Scientologists providing most of the money and manpower.

ECT Saves Lives

To the public, ECT may seem too drastic a treatment for "merely" psychological problems. But the illnesses against which ECT is used are extremely serious. At worst, they are lethal—the suicide rate for patients with depression in the U.S. has been estimated at 15 percent. At best, they cause enormous suffering. In surveys, individuals with both a history of severe depression and a history of physical trauma due to an accident ranked the pain of mental illness as much worse than that of physical trauma. Schizophrenia is even more devastating. As one psychiatrist has observed, "Schizophrenia takes away the entire life of the person . . . it destroys the mind, it destroys the soul of a youth."

ECT can restore lives. Roland Kohloff, chief timpanist with the New York Philharmonic, suffers from severe recurrent depression but controls it with ECT. His son, a hospital inpatient for years because of schizophrenia, improved, according to Kohloff, "magically" with ECT. Kohloff has pointed out that the late world-renowned virtuoso Vladimir Horowitz, one of the greatest pianists of the 20th century, abandoned his career for a decade because of depression. ECT ultimately rescued him, and he resumed playing in public. Whether he forgot who had attended a family birth-day party held months before his treatment is not recorded. But, as Kohloff has observed, it is a fact that after treatment Horowitz played pieces whose playing required memorizing hundreds of thousands of notes. Clearly, the great pianist's memory had not been impaired.

"From the very beginning . . .
[electroconvulsive therapy] was known to
cause brain damage."

Electroconvulsive Therapy
Causes Severe Brain Damage

Peter R. Breggin

Electroconvulsive therapy (ECT)— in which pulsed electricity is sent through electrodes that have been placed on a patient's head, inducing a brief seizure—is a dangerous treatment that results in significant brain damage, contends Peter R. Breggin in the following viewpoint. He maintains that ECT is harmful because human beings do not suffer convulsions unless sufficient damage is inflicted to their brains. According to Breggin, patients who undergo this treatment often endure lasting amnesia and mental dysfunction. Breggin is a psychiatrist and the author of many books, including *Talking Back to Prozac* and *Toxic Psychiatry*.

As you read, consider the following questions:
1. In Breggin's opinion, how is modern ECT more dangerous than the older forms?
2. What were Max Fink's early views on ECT and cerebral trauma, as stated by the author?
3. According to Breggin, when does the therapeutic effect of ECT evaporate?

Excerpted from "Electroshock: Scientific, Ethical, and Political Issues," by Peter R. Breggin, *International Journal of Risk & Safety in Medicine*, June 1998. Reprinted with the permission of IOS Press, Inc.

For the past two to three decades, a modified form of electroconvulsive therapy (ECT) has been commonly (but not exclusively) used in the United States. It involves sedation with a short-acting intravenous barbiturate, followed by muscle paralysis with a curare derivative, and artificial respiration with oxygen to compensate for the paralysis of the patient's breathing musculature. The purpose of these modifications was not, as some advocates claim, to reduce memory loss and brain damage. Muscle paralysis was intended to prevent fractures of the spine and limbs, as well cracked teeth, from severe muscle spasms. The artificial respiration was added to keep the paralyzed patient oxygenated.

The modifications used in contemporary ECT make clear that ECT-induced convulsions are far more severe than the spontaneous convulsions in grand mal epilepsy. Patients with seizures of unknown origin, or with seizures due to brain injury, rarely break their limbs or their vertebrae during the convulsion. The muscle spasms are not intense enough to produce these effects. Yet these fractures were common with unmodified ECT.

ECT advocates commonly claim that recent modifications have made the treatment much safer, and that its negative public image is unfairly based on the older methods. However, the most basic modifications—anesthesia, muscle paralysis, and artificial respiration—are not new at all. I prescribed and administered such modified treatment more than thirty years ago (1963/64) as a resident at Harvard Medical School's main psychiatric teaching facility, the Massachusetts Mental Health Center.

Modern ECT Is Dangerous

The public's "mistaken" image of ECT is, in reality, based on modern modified ECT, which has been around for a long time. It is actually more dangerous than the older forms. The electric currents must be more intense in order to overcome the anticonvulsant effects of the sedatives that are given during modified ECT. Too frequently, the patient is routinely given a sleeping medication or tranquilizer the night before, further increasing the brain's resistance to having a seizure. In addition, the patient is exposed to the added risk of anesthesia. Other modifications include changes in the type of electrical energy employed and the use of unilateral shocks applied to the non dominant (nonverbal) side of the brain. However, these modifications remain controversial. Since the APA task force does not exclusively endorse nondominant (unilateral) ECT, the claim that this method is much safer becomes moot. Bilateral ECT continues to be used around the world. Besides, as already described, some ECT advocates give excessive electrical doses—beyond the dose required to produce a convulsion.

There is no reason to believe that shocking the nonverbal side of the brain is less harmful. As [Thomas] Blakeslee has confirmed, damage and dysfunction on the nonverbal side are more difficult to recognize or to describe (see discussion of anosognosia ahead). But the defects are no less devastating. Injury to the nonverbal side impairs visual memory, spatial relations, musical and artistic abilities, judgment, insight, intuition, and personality. It is ironic that biopsychiatry promotes sacrificing the nonverbal side of the brain, while humanistic psychology is emphasizing its importance to the full development of human potential.

No matter how ECT is modified, one fact is inescapable: evolution has assured that human beings do not easily fall victim to convulsions. Therefore sufficient damage must be inflicted to overcome the brain's protective systems.

ECT Leads to Brain Damage

At the time that ECT was first developed, it was thought that convulsions induced by a variety of methods, including insulin coma and stimulant medication, were useful in treating psychiatric disorders, especially schizophrenia. It was often assumed that these treatments had their therapeutic effect by causing significant microscopic brain damage. Some advocates openly called for inducing brain damage and dysfunction. [Lucio] Bini, for example, reported that ECT produced "widespread and severe" neuropathology in the brain and that these "alterations" might be responsible for the "transformation" seen in schizophrenic patients after ECT. [In 1938, psychiatrist] Roy Grinker compared ECT to lobotomy and speculated, "Does shock therapy improve schizophrenic patients by structural damage of a less intense but more diffuse type?" In 1941 Walter Freeman wrote an editorial entitled "Brain Damaging Therapeutics" in which he argued for the basic principle that the major psychiatric treatments, including electroshock and lobotomy, work by disabling brain function. In 1941, Harry Solomon's introduction to [Lucie] Jessner and [V. Gerard] Ryan's *Shock Treatment in Psychiatry* acknowledged that ECT produces memory loss, brain wave changes, and "cerebral cellular damage and vascular injury." He connected this to the therapeutic effect, specifically the production of euphoria and hypomania. The textbook itself cited evidence for severe brain damage from ECT, including "capillary hemorrhage, ganglion cell changes, consisting of swelling and shrinkage, satellitosis, gliosis and demyelinization."

Long-Term/Permanent Mental Effects Following ECT

	SLIGHT	MODERATE	SEVERE
Loss of past memories	8%	33%	41%
Impaired present memory	9%	36%	36%
Impaired concentration	8%	35%	42%
Impaired organization skills	9%	27%	30%
Impaired number skills	11%	25%	15%
Impaired language/writing	8%	31%	21%
Panic attacks	11%	25%	21%
Bad dreams or nightmares	11%	20%	22%
Feelings of remoteness	6%	26%	30%
Personality changes	8%	22%	32%
Fear of doctors & hospitals	10%	17%	37%
Agoraphobia	4%	12%	10%
Claustrophobia	7%	14%	10%
Suicidal Tendencies	10%	20%	22%

"Shock-Treatment Damage Survey," *ECT Anonymous*, March 1999. Found at http://members.aol.com/wmacdo4301/electro/papers/equest1.htm

From the very beginning—based on animal studies, human autopsies, and clinical observation—ECT was known to cause brain damage. In fact, the brain damage was considered the principal element of the therapeutic impact. Later, with increasing concern about ECT's bad image, advocates began to deny these well-established observations.

Max Fink is a leader in promoting ECT and his attitudes, if sometimes more extreme, reflect those of many others who are leading the current resurgence of ECT in North America and Europe. A pro-ECT review by another ECT advocate, Richard Wiener, drew from Fink accusations that Wiener "genuflects to avoid criticism" and that "such kowtowing is inappropriate."

Fink, himself a member of the 1978 and 1990 American Psychiatric Association (APA) task forces, for decades argued and demonstrated scientifically that ECT's "therapeutic" effect is produced by brain dysfunction and damage. He pointed out in his 1974 textbook [*Psychobiology of Convulsive Therapy*] that "patients become more compliant and acquiescent with treatment." He connected the so-called improvement with "denial," "disorientation," and other signs of traumatic brain injury and an organic brain syndrome.

Fink was even more explicit in earlier studies. In 1957, he stated that the basis for improvement from ECT is "craniocerebral trauma." In 1966, Fink cited research indicating that after ECT "the behavioral changes related to the degree of induced trauma. . . ." Referring to the multiple abnormalities produced in the brain following ECT, Fink wrote "In these regards, induced convulsions in man are more similar to cerebral trauma than to spontaneous seizures." He stated that improvement depends on the development of an abnormal EEG and other changes in the brain and spinal fluid typical of trauma and compared ECT to "cerebral trauma."

Fink cited [Donald B.] Tower and [D.] McEachern, correctly stating that they "concluded that spinal fluid changes in induced convulsions were more like those of craniocerebral trauma than those of spontaneous epilepsy." He then gave further evidence for this comparison between ECT and traumatic brain injury.

Further Indications of Brain Damage

As recently as 1974, Fink continued to propose that ECT has its effect by traumatizing or damaging the brain. He begins his discussion by noting that psychiatric "treatments have been often drastic" and then cites, among other examples, heat and burning, bleeding, water immersion, and craniotomy. He then goes on to present several axioms of ECT, including the connection between the supposed therapeutic effect and traumatic changes in the brain. He speaks directly of the producing "cerebral trauma" reflected in EEG slow wave activity. He compares induced convulsions to "craniocerebral trauma." He attributes improvement to the increased use of "denial" by the patient and to the development of "hypomania"—both signs of profound irrationality caused by brain damage and dysfunction.

The 1990 task force report, despite Fink's participation, made no such comparisons between head injury and ECT; instead the report dismissed any suggestion that the treatment is significantly traumatic. In depositions in defense of doctors who give ECT, Fink now takes the position that ECT causes no brain damage.

The 1990 APA task force report notes that low-dose unilateral ECT is often less effective than forms of ECT that deliver more electrical energy. This observation tends to confirm the brain-disabling principle that efficacy depends on the degree of damage.

More recently [Harold] Sackeim and Sackeim with a team of colleagues have covertly revived the principle that a therapeutic response depends upon the degree of brain damage and dysfunction. Sackeim has found that "Regardless of electrode placement, patients who received high dosage treatments responded more quickly . . . Critically, we also found that the rate of clinical response was dosage sensitive." As previously noted, the degree of post-ECT disorientation and later retrograde amnesia is also dose sensitive.

[Another study] used the suprathreshold dose (2.5 times) in a group of patients in a crossover study. This group suffered from massive retrograde amnesia that did not improve two months after ECT.

Loss of Memory and Identity

I evaluated a case in which a doctor followed Sackeim's published recommendation and gave his patient the increased dosage. The patient suffered severe, irreversible memory loss and chronic mental dysfunction, rendering her permanently unable to work at her previous high intellectual level.

The tendency to increase the electrical dose wholly undermines the promotional campaign aimed at convincing the public that modern electroshock is safer. Sackeim and his colleagues often use bilateral ECT—the most obviously damaging method—with a dose of electricity 2.5 times that required to produce a convulsion in the patient. In addition, a growing emphasis on continuation or maintenance ECT will expose increasing numbers of patients to chronic brain trauma and dysfunction.

More striking, Sackeim wants to do away with the safety features currently placed on most ECT machines that limit current intensity: "These upper limits result in clinicians resorting to unnecessary and perhaps risky maneuvers. . . ." to get higher doses. According to Sackeim, "In my view, a strong argument can be made that the next generation of ECT devices have significantly higher upper output limits, perhaps at least double what is available with the current generation."

In a recent issue of *Convulsive Therapy*, ECT advocate Charles Kellner quotes a description of shock-induced mental devastation written by survivor "Ellen Wolfe." Mrs Wolfe describes the "muddles" she gets into reading and her inability to recall even dramatic life events, such as the assassination of President Kennedy. Kellner states that her tragic outcome, "a very severe case," is "likely the result of a series of treatments with high-dose bilateral sine wave ECT." Without seeming to realize that modern ECT is often more "high-dose" than the older methods, he states that such a tragic outcome is unlikely with contemporary ECT. This view contrasts sharply with his more cautionary words:

> Memory is often equated with the very essence of a person's "being." As such, discussions about ECT's effects on memory deserve our most careful consideration.

Helplessness and Denial

ECT provides a prototype for the concept of iatrogenic [doctor-induced] helplessness and denial. Controlled studies of ECT show that any therapeutic effect evaporates after 4 weeks, the approximate time it takes to recover from the most severe symptoms of the organic brain syndrome or delirium. Except for psychosurgery, ECT provides the most extreme example in which the psychiatrist denies the damage he is doing to the patient, and then utilizes the effects of that damage to produce less emotionally aware, less autonomous, and more manageable patients. As Max Fink used to openly describe, brain damage and the exercise of medical authority push patients into denial about the harm done to them as well as about their still unresolved personal problems.

Consistent with other victims of central nervous system damage, most ECT patients minimize or deny their real losses of mental function. This denial of mental dysfunction in brain-damaged patients is called anosognosia. C.M. Fisher considers anosognosia or denial of dysfunction to be a hallmark of brain injury: "Unawareness accompanies so many neurologic defects that one might invoke anosognosia as a broad principle of cerebral dysfunction in humans." I have pointed out that it should be considered an integral part of the brain-disabling effects of all psychiatric treatments which impair brain function. Brain-disabling treatments reduce the patient's awareness of the mental dysfunction caused by the treatment.

While damage to either side of the brain can produce anosognosia, it seems more common following damage to the nondominant side (in right-handed individuals, the right is usually nondominant). In electroshock treatment, at least one electrode lies over the nondominant side. In contemporary ECT, both electrodes are frequently placed over the nondominant side.

Nondominant electroshock starkly illustrates the principle of iatrogenic helplessness and denial: the doctor damages the brain in such a way as to confound the patient's ability to perceive the resulting dysfunction. Neurologically informed advocates of ECT are well aware that electroshock patients end up suffering from anosognosia and denial, and therefore cannot fully report the extent of their memory losses and mental dysfunction. Yet these same advocates claim that patients exaggerate their post-ECT problems.

Interviews with family and friends of patients often disclose that they are painfully aware of the damage done to their loved ones. Often, the psychiatrist is the only one who consistently and unequivocally denies the patient's damaged state. . . .

The Personal Cost to Survivors

It is impossible to find words that are sufficient to communicate the tragic personal cost to many of the patients who undergo ECT. In my own experience, spanning more than thirty years, I have encountered dozens of individuals whose lives have been wrecked by the effects of ECT on their mental function. Many have been left with such devastating retrograde amnesia that they can no longer function as professional persons or homemakers. Years of professional training and other key aspects of their lives have been obliterated. Even portions of their past that they can remember may seem remote and alien as if they are watching a movie rather than recalling their own lives. Often they have been impaired in their ongoing ability to focus or pay attention, to concentrate, to make sense out of complex situations, to remember names and places, to learn anything new, to find their way around, and to read and think effectively. Frequently they have become irritable and easily frustrated, emotionally unstable, and shallow in their ability to feel. Often they feel depressed and even suicidal over the loss of their mental function. In short, they have shown all the typical signs of close-head injury, including frontal and temporal lobe dysfunction. Often their families have been irreparably damaged by their inability to function as wage earners, husbands or wives, mothers or fathers. A treatment that can cause such devastation, while producing such limited and questionable results, has no place in the practice of medicine.

Periodical Bibliography

The following articles have been selected to supplement the diverse views presented in this chapter. Addresses are provided for periodicals not indexed in the *Readers' Guide to Periodical Literature*, the *Alternative Press Index*, the *Social Sciences Index*, or the *Index to Legal Periodicals and Books*.

Natalie Angier	"Drugs for Depression Multiply, and So Do the Hard Questions," *New York Times*, June 22, 1997.
Irene Barrett	"Right Before My Eyes," *Natural Health*, November/December 1996. Available from Weider Publications, 21100 Erwin St., Woodland Hills, CA 91367.
Michael Castleman	"Becoming Unblued," *Mother Jones*, May/June 1997.
Jeff Cohen and Norman Solomon	"Electroshock Gets Powerful Boost from Media," *Liberal Opinion Week*, June 12, 1995. Available from PO Box 880, Vinton, IA 52349-0880.
Mark S. Gold	"Know Your SSRIs: The Ups and Downs of Antidepressants," *Professional Counselor*, October 1997. Available from 3201 SW 15th St., Deerfield Beach, FL 33442-8190.
Kevin Heldman	"7½ Days," *City Limits*, June/July 1998.
Scott O. Lilienfeld	"EMDR Treatment: Less Than Meets the Eye?" *Skeptical Inquirer*, January/February 1996.
Peter Lomas	"The Durability of the Talking Cure," *Society*, November/December 1997.
Scott D. Miller, Mark A. Hubble, and Barry L. Duncan	"Counseling for Change," *Professional Counselor*, February 1997.
Sue Miller	"A Natural Mood Booster," *Newsweek*, May 5, 1997.
Anuradha Raghunathan	"A Bold Rush to Sell Drugs to the Shy," *New York Times*, May 18, 1999.
Victoria Secunda	"Emotional Upsets? Suffer No More!" *New Choices*, May 1997.
Laura Wexler	"Thinking, Not Shrinking," *Utne Reader*, January/February 1997.
Michael Yapko	"Stronger Medicine," *Family Therapy Networker*, January/February 1997. Available from Family Therapy Network, 7705 13th St., NW, Washington, DC 20012.

For Further Discussion

Chapter 1

1. L.J. Davis and Paula J. Caplan contend that the definition of what is considered a mental illness is too broad because it categorizes such behaviors as shyness, insomnia, sleepwalking, and premenstrual syndrome as mental disorders. The American Psychiatric Association maintains, however, that simply listing a disorder in the *Diagnostic and Statistical Manual of Mental Disorders* does not imply that the condition meets the legal criteria for mental illness. Explain why the APA might list such behaviors in the DSM if they are not mental diseases. What conditions do you think qualify as mental illnesses?

2. According to Hillary Rodham Clinton and Steven Hyman, mental illnesses are diseases of the brain and should be treated the same as other medical disorders. Martin Bobgan and Deidre Bobgan disagree, arguing that mental illness is not a disease because the mind is not a physical organ and therefore cannot be physically sick or damaged. Whose argument do you find more convincing and why?

3. Using the case of a man who confessed to killing his own daughter but was not judged harshly by most members of his online support group, Dennis Prager concludes that many people are too quick to excuse immoral behavior by labeling it a symptom of mental illness. Do you agree with his conclusion or do you think the example he used is too atypical to apply to a more general theory? Explain your answer.

Chapter 2

1. After reading the viewpoints by E. Fuller Torrey and Ira A. Burnim, do you think that institutions have helped or harmed the mentally ill? Explain your answers.

2. Do you agree with Richard E. Vatz's contention that insurance should cover only the most severe mental illnesses, or do you agree with Lewis L. Judd that mental illness should be treated no differently than physical health problems? Explain your answers.

3. Based on the viewpoints in this chapter and any other relevant material, do you think that society does too much or too little to accommodate the needs of people diagnosed with mental illnesses? What, if any, accommodations do you feel should be added or eliminated? Explain your answers.

Chapter 3

1. Thomas Armstrong contends that the extent of attention deficit disorder is exaggerated. Based on your reading of the viewpoints, do you believe this childhood disorder is widespread or overdiagnosed? Support your answer.

2. Arianna Huffington fears that parents and teachers want to drug children to more easily control normal childhood behavior. Do you agree with her contention? Why or why not? How does Harold S. Koplewicz respond to Huffington's argument?

3. Russell A. Barkley, George J. DuPaul, and Anthony Costello assert that Ritalin is safe and effective for children with attention deficit disorder. Mary Eberstadt contends, however, that Ritalin is too similar to cocaine and other dangerous drugs to be used safely. Which argument is stronger? Explain your answer. Do the authors' backgrounds influence your assessment of their arguments? Why or why not?

Chapter 4

1. *Consumer Reports* is a nonprofit and impartial consumer magazine that does not have ties to the mental health industry. Based on those factors, do you put more or less credence into its survey and conclusions? Would you be more likely to agree with a survey conducted by a magazine that focuses exclusively on mental illness? Explain your answers.

2. Do you agree with Al Siebert's contention that psychiatrists and psychologists consider everyone to be mentally ill? Why or why not?

3. Rael Jean Isaac and Peter Breggin offer different perspectives on electroconvulsive therapy's effect on memory. Whose argument do you find more convincing and why?

Organizations to Contact

The editors have compiled the following list of organizations concerned with the issues debated in this book. The descriptions are derived from materials provided by the organizations. All have publications or information available for interested readers. The list was compiled on the date of publication of the present volume; the information provided here may change. Be aware that many organizations take several weeks or longer to respond to inquiries, so allow as much time as possible.

American Psychiatric Association (APA)
1400 K St. NW, Washington, DC 20005
(202) 682-6000 • fax: (202) 682-6850
e-mail: apa@psych.org • website: http://www.psych.org
An organization of psychiatrists dedicated to studying the nature, treatment, and prevention of mental disorders, the APA helps create mental health policies, distributes information about psychiatry, and promotes psychiatric research and education. It publishes the *American Journal of Psychiatry* monthly and the pamphlet *Delirium: A Patient and Family Guide.*

American Psychological Association (APA)
750 First St. NE, Washington, DC 20002-4242
(202) 336-5500 • fax: (202) 336-5708
e-mail: public.affairs@apa.org • website: http://www.apa.org
The American Psychological Association is the world's largest association of psychologists. It produces numerous publications, including *Acute Stress Disorder: A Handbook of Theory, Assessment, and Treatment* and *Sexuality, Society, and Feminism.*

Canadian Mental Health Association (CMHA)
2160 Yonge St., 3rd Floor, Toronto, ON M4S 2Z3 Canada
(416) 484-7750 • fax: (416) 484-4617
e-mail: cmhanat@interlog.com • website: http://www.cmha.ca
The Canadian Mental Health Association assists people suffering from mental illness in finding the help they need to cope with crises, regain confidence, and return to their communities, families, and jobs. It publishes the pamphlets *Children and Attention Deficit Disorders, The Myths of Mental Illness,* and *Depression and Manic Depression.*

Children and Adults with Attention-Deficit/Hyperactivity Disorder (CHADD)
8181 Professional Place, Suite 201, Landover, MD 20785
(800) 233-4050 • (301) 306-7070 • fax (301) 306-7090
e-mail: national@chadd.org • website: http://www.chadd.org

CHADD was founded by parents who work to improve the lives of children and adults with attention-deficit/hyperactivity disorder through education, advocacy, and support. It publishes the quarterly *Attention!* magazine, books, and the fact sheets "Disability Named ADD" and "Controversial Treatment."

Citizens Commission on Human Rights (CCHR)
6362 Hollywood Blvd., Los Angeles, CA 90028
(800) 869-2217 • (213) 467-4242 • fax (213) 467-3720
e-mail: humanrights@cchr.org • website: http://www.cchr.org

CCHR works to expose and eradicate criminal acts and human rights abuses by psychiatry. The organization believes that psychiatric drugs cause insanity and violence. CCHR publishes the books *Psychiatry: Destroying Morals* and *Psychiatry: Education's Ruin.*

National Alliance for the Mentally Ill (NAMI)
200 N. Glebe Rd., Suite 1015, Arlington, VA 22203-3754
(800) 950-6264 • fax: (703) 524-9094
website: http://www.nami.org

NAMI is a consumer advocacy and support organization that believes that severe mental illnesses are biological brain diseases and that mentally ill people should not be blamed or stigmatized for their condition. Its publications include the bimonthly newsletter *NAMI Advocate* and the book *Breakthroughs in Antipsychotic Medications.*

National Alliance for Research on Schizophrenia and Depression (NARSAD)
60 Cutter Mill Rd., Suite 404, Great Neck, NY 11021
(516) 829-0091 • fax: (516) 487-6930
website: http://www.mhsource.com/narsad.html

The alliance is a nonprofit coalition of citizens' groups that raises funds for research into the causes, treatments, cures, and prevention of severe mental illnesses. It publishes *NARSAD Research*, a quarterly newsletter.

National Association of Psychiatric Survivors (NAPS)
PO Box 618, Sioux Falls, SD 57101
(605) 334-4067

The association opposes involuntary psychiatric procedures such as civil commitment and forced treatment. Instead, it advocates the rights of the mentally ill to choose their own treatments and to refuse unwanted treatments. It publishes the quarterly newsletter *NAPS/News*.

National Depressive and Manic Depressive Association (NDMDA)

730 N. Franklin St., Suite 501, Chicago, IL 60610-3526
(800) 826-3632 • (312) 642-0049 • fax: (312) 642-7243
e-mail: arobinson@ndmda.org • website: http://www.ndmda.org

The association provides support and advocacy for patients with depression and manic-depressive illness. It believes these disorders are biochemical in nature and that no stigmatization should be placed on the people who suffer from them. It publishes the quarterly *NDMDA Newsletter* and the books *Electro-Convulsive Therapy: A Guide* and *Finding Peace of Mind: Medication Strategies for Depression.*

National Foundation for Depressive Illness (NAFDI)

PO Box 2257, New York, NY 10116
(800) 239-1265
website: http://www.depression.org

NAFDI provides information about depression and manic-depressive illness. It believes that these disorders are treatable with medication, and that such medication should be made readily available to those who need it. The foundation publishes the quarterly newsletter *NAFDI News* and the fact sheet "Symptoms of Depression and Manic Depression."

National Mental Health Association (NMHA)

1021 Prince St., Alexandria, VA 2231-2971
(703) 684-7722 • fax: (703) 684-5968
e-mail: nmhainfo@aol.com • website: http://www.nmha.org

The association is a consumer advocacy organization that promotes research into the treatment and prevention of mental illness, monitors the quality of care provided to the mentally ill, and provides educational materials on mental illness and mental health. It publishes the monthly newsletter *The Bell*, books, and the pamphlets *Mental Health and You* and *Stigma: Awareness and Understanding of Mental Illness.*

Obsessive-Compulsive Foundation (OCF)

337 Notch Hill Rd., North Branford, CT 06471
(203) 315-2190 • fax: (203) 315-2196
e-mail: info@ocfoundation.org
website: http://www.ocfoundation.org

The foundation works to increase public awareness of and discover a cure for obsessive-compulsive disorders. It publishes the bimonthly *OCD Newsletter* and the pamphlet *OCD Questions and Answers.*

Bibliography of Books

Colleen Alexander-Roberts and Mark Snyder — *Does My Child Need a Therapist?* Dallas: Taylor Publishing, 1997.

Thomas Armstrong — *The Myth of the A.D.D. Child: 50 Ways to Improve Your Child's Behavior and Attention Span Without Drugs, Labels, or Coercion.* New York: Dutton, 1995.

Russell A. Barkley — *Taking Charge of ADHD: The Complete, Authoritative Guide for Parents.* New York: The Guilford Press, 1995.

Peter R. Breggin — *Talking Back to Ritalin: What Doctors Aren't Telling You About Stimulants for Children.* Monroe, ME: Common Courage Press, 1998.

Paula J. Caplan — *They Say You're Crazy: How the World's Most Powerful Psychiatrists Decide Who Is Normal.* Reading, MA: Addison-Wesley, 1995.

Elizabeth Russell Connelly — *Conduct Unbecoming: Hyperactivity, Attention Deficit, and Disruptive Behavior Disorders.* Philadelphia: Chelsea House Publishers, 1999.

Leon Cytryn and Donald H. McKnew — *Growing Up Sad: Childhood Depression and Its Treatment.* New York: Norton, 1996.

Todd Davison — *Life After Psychotherapy.* Northvale, NJ: Jason Aronson, 1997.

Richard J. DeGrandpre — *Ritalin Nation: Rapid-Fire Culture and the Transformation of Human Consciousness.* New York: W.W. Norton, 1999.

Robert Desjarlais — *Shelter Blues: Sanity and Selfhood Among the Homeless.* Philadelphia: University of Pennsylvania Press, 1997.

Kathleen DesMaisons — *Potatoes Not Prozac: A Natural Seven-Step Dietary Plan to Stabilize the Level of Sugar in Your Blood, Control Your Cravings and Lose Weight, and Recognize How Foods Affect the Way You Feel.* New York: Simon & Schuster, 1998.

Lawrence H. Diller — *Running on Ritalin: A Physician Reflects on Children, Society, and Performance in a Pill.* New York: Bantam Books, 1998.

Debra Elfenbein, ed. — *Living With Prozac and Other Selective Serotonin Reuptake Inhibitors (SSRIs): Personal Accounts of Life on Antidepressants.* San Francisco: HarperSan Francisco, 1995.

Robert T. Fancher — *Cultures of Healing: Correcting the Image of American Mental Health Care.* New York: W.H. Freeman and Company, 1995.

Stephen W. Garber, Marianne Daniels Garber, and Robyn Freedman Spizman — *Beyond Ritalin: Facts About Medication and Other Strategies for Helping Children, Adolescents, and Adults With Attention Deficit Disorders.* New York: Villard, 1996.

Thom Hartmann — *Beyond ADD: Hunting for Reasons in the Past and Present.* Grass Valley, CA: Underwood Books, 1996.

Barbara D. Ingersoll and Sam Goldstein — *Lonely, Sad and Angry: A Parent's Guide to Depression in Children and Adolescents.* New York: Doubleday, 1995.

Kay Redfield Jamison — *An Unquiet Mind.* New York: Alfred A. Knopf, 1995.

David A. Karp — *Speaking of Sadness: Depression, Disconnection, and the Meanings of Illness.* New York: Oxford University Press, 1996.

Harold S. Koplewicz — *It's Nobody's Fault: New Hope and Help for Difficult Children and Their Parents.* New York: Times Books, 1996.

Herb Kutchins — *Making Us Crazy: DSM: The Psychiatric Bible and the Creation of Mental Disorders.* New York: Free Press, 1997.

Elaine McEwan — *Managing Attention & Learning Disorders: Super Survival Strategies.* Wheaton, IL: Harold Shaw Publishers, 1997.

Michael J. Norden — *Beyond Prozac: Brain-Toxic Lifestyles, Natural Antidotes & New Generation Antidepressants.* New York: Regan Books, 1995.

Helen C. Packard — *Prozac: The Controversial Cure.* New York: Rosen Publishing Group, 1998.

Laurel Parnell — *Transforming Trauma—EMDR: The Revolutionary New Therapy for Freeing the Mind, Clearing the Body, and Opening the Heart.* New York: W.W. Norton, 1997.

John J. Ratey and Catherine Johnson — *Shadow Syndromes.* New York: Pantheon Books, 1997.

Terrence Real — *I Don't Want to Talk About It: Overcoming the Secret Legacy of Male Depression.* New York: Scribner, 1997.

Norman Rosenthal — *St. John's Wort: The Herbal Way to Feeling Good.* New York: HarperCollins, 1998.

Judith Sachs	*Nature's Prozac: Natural Therapies and Techniques To Rid Yourself of Anxiety, Depression, Panic Attacks, & Stress.* Englewood Cliffs, NJ: Prentice Hall, 1997.
Francine Shapiro and Margot Silk Forrest	*EMDR: The Breakthrough Therapy for Overcoming Anxiety, Stress, and Trauma.* New York: BasicBooks, 1997.
Edward Shorter	*A History of Psychiatry: From the Era of the Asylum to the Age of Prozac.* New York: John Wiley & Sons, 1997.
Stephen R. Shuchter, Nancy Downs, and Sidney Zisook	*Biologically Informed Psychotherapy for Depression.* New York: The Guilford Press, 1996.
Lauren Slater	*Prozac Diary.* New York: Random House, 1998.
E. Fuller Torrey	*Out of the Shadows: Confronting America's Mental Illness Crisis.* New York: John Wiley & Sons, 1997.
Carol A. Turkington	*The Hypericum Handbook: Using St. John's Wort, "Nature's Prozac," To Alleviate Depression.* New York: M. Evans and Company, 1998.
Abraham J. Twerski	*Getting Up When You're Down: A Mature Discussion of an Adult Malady—Depression and Related Conditions.* Brooklyn, NY: Shaar Press, 1997.
Elliot S. Valenstein	*Blaming the Brain: The Truth About Drugs and Mental Health.* New York: Free Press, 1998.
Peter C. Whybrow	*A Mood Apart: Depression, Mania, and Other Afflictions of the Self.* New York: BasicBooks, 1997.
Charles V. Willie, Patricia Perri Rieker, Bernard M. Kramer, and Bertram S. Brown	*Mental Health, Racism, and Sexism.* Pittsburgh: University of Pittsburgh Press, 1995.
Michael D. Yapko	*Breaking the Patterns of Depression.* New York: Doubleday, 1997.

Index